AMBIGUITY IN NATURAL LANGUAGE

An investigation of certain pro

NORTH-HOLLAND
LINGUISTIC SERIES   3
Edited by S. C. DIK and J. G. KOOIJ

AMBIGUITY IN NATURAL LANGUAGE

An investigation of certain problems in its linguistic description

JAN G. KOOIJ

Institute for General Linguistics
University of Amsterdam

1971

NORTH-HOLLAND PUBLISHING COMPANY
AMSTERDAM · LONDON

Library of Congress Catalog Card Number:

ISBN: 0 7204 6184 7

Publisher:
NORTH-HOLLAND PUBLISHING COMPANY – AMSTERDAM

PRINTED IN THE NETHERLANDS

to the memory of my mother
to my father and Tine

τὰ μὲν γὰρ ᾽ονόματα πεπέρανται
καὶ τὸ τῶν λόγων πλῆθος, τὰ
δὲ πράγματα τὸν ἀριθμὸν ἄπειρά
᾽εστιν. ᾽αναγκαῖον οὖν πλείω
τὸν αὐτον λόγον καὶ τοὔνομα
τὸ ἕν σημαίνειν.

'For names are finite and so is the sum-total
of formulae, while things are infinite in
number. Inevitably, then, the same formula,
and a single name, have a number of meanings'

Aristotle, *De sophisticis elenchis*

PREFACE

This book is an informal discussion of certain problems connected with the linguistic description of ambiguity.

It owes much to Professor Anton Reichling, under whose supervision it was prepared, and submitted as a doctoral thesis to the Faculty of Arts of the University of Amsterdam. I have been continually inspired by his views on natural language, and by the way these were put forward in his lectures and discussed on many other occasions. I have profited also from his frank and detailed criticisms of earlier versions of this study.

I am much indebted also to my colleagues Professor Simon C. Dik and Mr. Norval S.H. Smith, who contributed invaluable improvements in content and style of this book. Remaining errors and weaknesses are mine.

I am obliged to all those who have, in various ways, assisted and encouraged me in the writing of this book: by providing me with preprints or reprints of publications and other information, by discussing the subject matter with me, and by listening to and not being bored by examples of ambiguities. I mention here: Professor Yuen Ren Chao, Mr. Robert S. Kirsner, Drs. R. Landheer, Dr. Q.I.M. Mok, and colleagues and students in the Institute for General Linguistics of the University of Amsterdam.

I am grateful to various people in the Institute for their most generous assistance in the completion of the manuscript, and to the management and staff of the North-Holland Publishing Company for patience and efficiency.

Amsterdam, January 1971   Jan G. Kooij

CONTENTS

1. AMBIGUITY IN NATURAL LANGUAGE

1.1. Preliminary remarks

The scope of the term 'ambiguity' is rather wide, but may be narrowed down for certain purposes. In everyday usage, 'ambiguity' usually refers to the property of sentences that they may be interpreted in more than one way and that insufficient clues are available for the intended or the optimal interpretation. The term ambiguity is then synonymous with 'lack of clarity' or 'equivocation', a phenomenon that can be looked upon as a shortcoming of language users, as a deficiency of the system of natural language, or both. The various aspects of ambiguity in this sense have been succinctly summarized by Kaplan (1950:1):

'Ambiguity is the common cold of the pathology of language. The logician recognizes equivocation as a frequent source of fallacious reasoning. The student of propaganda and public opinion sees in ambiguity an enormous obstacle to successful communication. Even the sciences are not altogether free of verbalistic disputes that turn on confused multiple meanings of key terms in the controversy.'

In fact, both in the past and in the present, ambiguity has been first and foremost discussed in a pragmatic context, although theoretical observations on ambiguity as a phenomenon of natural language are not always absent in such discussions. For instance, a penetrating discussion of ambiguity can be found in various writings of Aristotle, especially in his *De sophisticis elenchis*. His main purpose, however, appears to have been to expose ambiguity in the sense of 'fallacious reasoning' in philosophical disputes[1], and to point out the fact that one and the same sentence may contain, or perhaps one should say conceal, more than one 'proposition'. In *Ars rhetorica* (1404a 38) he goes as far as to state that homonymy in the sense of the deliberate use of homonymous terms in speech and writing is the form of communication habitual with sophists, whereas for poets it is synonymy, by which in that context he means the motivated use of one and the same 'term' for different 'things', or,

---

[1] A stock example in this connection is the equivocation of the expression 'Law of nature' (see, e.g., Black 1952:170). Since a law is generally understood to be 'made' by somebody or at least on somebody's orders, the expression 'Law of nature' could therefore seem to imply that there must be 'somebody' who rules nature too.

the metaphorical use of the language. Quintilian (*Institutio Oratoria* VI:3,46 ff.), whose discussion of ambiguity is far less original, considers it above all as a device frequently used and abused in courtrooms; the remarks he makes in that connection on Cicero's reputation for this, would seem to imply that Quintilian is not in favour of it.

The aims of the 17th century French linguist Vaugelas (see Mok 1968b) in his discussion of 'équivoque' are also in the first place practical. He scorns 'constructions lousches' to be found in sentences such as

la fille du fermier qui nous vend des légumes

where the relative *qui* can have either *fille* or *fermier* as its antecedent, and he gives prescriptions to avoid this kind of ambiguity in speaking and writing. Similar examples reappear in Bally 1944[2].

As a matter of fact, the various 'types' of ambiguity usually mentioned in current linguistic textbooks are not altogether new if one compares them with what is to be found in older books, and few of them are as elaborate as Aristotle's.

In *De sophisticis elenchis* (165 ff.), he mentions six 'ways of producing the false appearance of an argument which depend on language'. Among them are ὁμωνυμία, lexical ambiguity of words; ἀμφιβολία, constructional homonymy that arises through establishing the wrong grammatical relations, and two related, but distinguished types which have their source in constituent structure: σύνθεσις, wrong combination of elements, and διαίρεσις, wrong division of elements. His example of this fourth type is the sentence

τὰ πέντ' ἐστὶ δύο καὶ τρία

which of course should mean 'five is two plus three', but could also be taken to mean 'five is two and five is three', if one were to overlook that the division should be made between ἐστὶ and δύο καὶ τρία. Both the example and Aristotle's explanation of it recall recent discussions of ambiguity in coordination (see Dik 1968a:227).

After προσῳδία, 'accentuation', Aristotle has a sixth type of ambiguity, σχῆμα λέξεως, 'form of expression'. In *Topica* (15, 106b) this is illustrated as follows: 'To 'love' (τὸ φιλεῖν) also, used of the state of mind, has to 'hate' (τὸ μισεῖν) as its contrary, while as used of the physical activity it has none; clearly, therefore, to 'love' is an ambiguous term'.

The example and Aristotle's comments on it are interesting for several reasons. Firstly, because he draws attention to the non-equivalence of verbs that are similar morphologically and semi-equivalent syntactically, and secondly, because he views such a state of affairs (see also the discussion in *De so-*

phisticis elenchis) as a source of potential ambiguity in two ways: 'to love', as compared with 'to hate' and other verbs, has one sense more, and therefore is an ambiguous term; and on the other hand, somebody might, by false analogy, use the verb 'to hate' as if it could indicate an activity as well.

Other remarkable features of Aristotle's treatment of ambiguity are that he makes an explicit difference between words and sentences that have more than one meaning but are still the same, and cases of ambiguity where a sequence of elements represents two different 'sentences'. To this latter category would for instance belong the example of διαίρεσις given above. Also, in *De sophisticis elenchis* as well as in other books, Aristotle takes pains to explain that not all ambiguities in language use have their cause in an inherent ambiguity of linguistic elements.

To conclude this brief survey, it may be noted that Quintilian (o.c. chapter VII:9) gives some examples of ambiguous expressions that now would be regarded by some authors as disambiguated by 'juncture'. The sequence *in genua*, he says, could, at least theoretically, be interpreted as *in genua*, 'onto the knees' or as *ingenua*, 'freeborn woman'.

That the main topic of these discussions is the disadvantages of ambiguity and the ways to avoid it, rather than the phenomenon itself, does not mean that recent discussions of ambiguity do not find their inspiration in practical problems as well. Kaplan's study (1950) on the contextual resolution of ambiguity for instance, arose from the difficulties that ambiguity causes in the field of machine translation; other publications to be mentioned in this connection are Kuno and Oettinger 1963; Garvin 1968; Agricola 1968.

The discussion of ambiguity as a deficiency of the system of natural language has frequently led to a comparison between natural languages in this respect; also, to a comparison between natural language and other forms of communication: planned auxiliary languages, or formal languages like machine languages, or the calculi of mathematical logic. That natural language compares unfavorably to such systems has almost become a commonplace, since one of the goals in devising such a formal system *is* to define it unambiguously.

As for the comparison *between* natural languages, Jespersen (1964[12]:319–20) regards ambiguity as an inherent property of any natural language, but he does not want to rule out a priori the possibility that some languages could, in this respect, be less inadequate than other languages, or that ambiguities might increase with the development of a language, for instance with the loss of case-endings. Bally also feels that ambiguity is unavoidable (1944[2]:343), but about attempts to prove that one language is 'more clear' than another, he is sceptical (ibid. p.16). Bally — who can be mentioned as one of the not so many linguists who have paid ample attention to the ambiguity problem — on that occasion also expressed the view that ambiguity, though inherent to natural language, should not be overrated as an actual obstacle in communication: most ambiguities will automatically be resolved by verbal context or by the situation in general in which communication takes place. This, by now, is a quite readily accepted viewpoint (see for instance Kaplan 1950:1), which can be found also with authors who have a quite opposite view on the consequences of ambiguity for linguistic description (see Chomksy 1965:21; Reichling 1969[5]:100).

On the other hand, the phenomenon of 'multiple meaning' — whether accidental or intentional — is not always regarded as a negative feature even of language use. A well-known example of the positive view is Empson's study of poetry (1965:1). Here, the use of the terms 'ambiguous' and 'ambiguity' is mostly restricted to texts where the simultaneous presence of alternative meanings enhances the value of the text, or of its interpretation. Notice, however, that ambiguity in the field of literary criticism also, can be used in the negative, or at least the non-positive sense. In Booth 1966[6]:311 ff., 385 ff., novels are called 'ambiguous' when they leave the reader in uncertainty with respect to the standpoint of the author towards his characters, and this is considered by Booth as a major problem of evaluation rather than of interpretation.

1.2. Ambiguity and linguistics

Ambiguity in the sense of a disturbance in communication, or a device in communication, will not be the first concern of this book. The main subject of this study will be ambiguity as a property of sentences and its consequences for a linguistic description. In comparison to the different attitudes towards ambiguity briefly indicated above, the viewpoint taken in this study is neutral. To avoid possible misunderstandings: this only means a necessary restriction of scope, and is not meant to imply indifference towards the various social, literary or other communicative aspects of ambiguity in natural language, or towards natural language itself, for that matter. It is only assumed that for the purpose of a linguistic description disinterestedness should be the prevailing attitude.

It will, however, become progressively clear that ambiguity, even when the effects it can have, or the intentions that may be behind it are disregarded, is still connected with various aspects of language *use* that can*not* be disregarded so easily. Chao (1959:2) states that linguistics is the study of 'types' and philology the study of 'tokens' but adds the following comment in a foot-note: 'This is of course putting it very simply. Actually both disciplines deal with both kinds of problems and it is the difference in aim and emphasis which distinguishes the two'.

It can only be admitted that ambiguity is a subject which soon makes one aware of this difficulty. Even under the assumption that a linguistic study of ambiguity should start by restricting itself to the study of the inherent am-biguity of sentences and should as much as possible free itself from contextual and situational variables at that stage of the investigation, it cannot be over-looked that one is dealing with a system which is essentially a system for com-munication. Losing sight of this one runs a heavy risk of giving a distorted picture of what the problem is.

In order to restrict the scope of the term ambiguity as much as possible for the purposes of a linguistic description, let us provisionally define ambiguity as that property of a sentence that it can be interpreted in more than one way. For reasons to be discussed more extensively later (chapter 3, p. 58) I will understand by 'sentence' any sequence of linguistic elements to which at least one grammatical structure can be assigned and which has at least one meaning. Under this wide definition, the sentence

(1) Paul is coming to dinner tonight

would be ambiguous, since from this sentence alone one can not possibly infer who 'Paul' is, which might in some situations lead to confusion over who it is that is coming to dinner. Nevertheless, it can safely be assumed that not many linguists are willing to call a sentence like (1) above, ambiguous in itself for that reason[2], whereas many linguists would readily use the term to character-ize a sentence like

(2) The soldiers took the port at night[3]

in which *port* can mean 'harbour' or 'a kind of alcoholic beverage'.

It would appear, therefore, that for linguistic purposes one needs a distinc-tion between the ambiguity of sentences that, in abstraction from context and

---

[2] Though the 'ambiguity' of proper names is of course a legitimate subject of discus-sion, and in fact has been quite a common issue in philosophy; see e.g. Quine 1964[2], 27. According to Quintilian, the proper name *Ajax* is 'ambiguous', at least for literate people, since in the Iliad there are two people referred to by that name.

[3] The example is taken from MacKay and Bever 1967. Henceforth, the source of ex-amples will not be stated unless this is necessary for the discussion.

situation also, inherently have more than one meaning — such as (2) where *port* is a lexical homonym, and the ambiguity of sentences that do not have two meanings inherently but could still, in actual use, have more than one interpretation — such as (1). As pointed out by Gleason (1965:461–8), 'ambiguity' has in linguistics come to mean two quite different things, i.e.: (i) that a linguistic description assigns more than one structure, lexical or grammatical, to one and the same sentence, and (ii) that a sentence, though it has only one structure assigned to it, still can in some respect be insufficiently specified for communicative purposes. It may be added that this distinction is not at all easy to carry through consistently, and that in point of fact many discussions of ambiguity turn on exactly the question where to draw the line between 'inherent' and 'non-inherent' ambiguity. In this book I will act upon the assumption that it is one of the tasks of a linguistic description to try to find criteria for such a distinction.

A second distinction that is needed from the outset is the distinction between 'type' and 'token'. If ambiguity were to be investigated strictly from the communicative or textual point of view, it is clear that a sentence such as (2) above could be ambiguous on one occasion, but perfectly clear and unequivocal on another. To take into account these contextual and situational data would make the description of the ambiguity of sentences themselves virtually impossible, since their ambiguity would then vary with every situation where they are used. I would be inclined to say that even a study which aims at a description and explanation of contextual ambiguity will have to take the invariable properties of the sentences as its starting point. It will be understood that when a sentence from now on is said to be ambiguous what is meant is ambiguous as a type, not as an utterance-token in a uniquely defined speech situation. Notice that the distinction between ambiguous as a type, and ambiguous as a token, cuts through the distinction made earlier between 'inherent' and 'non-inherent' ambiguity: both (1) and (2) above may or may not be ambiguous as utterances, according to circumstances, though (2) but not (1) has inherently more than one meaning.

Finally, I wish to point out that the term 'ambiguous' will be used for sentences, and not, if it can be avoided, for all kinds of individual linguistic elements. In the literature, the same term 'ambiguous' and the related terms 'homonymous', 'homophonous', and 'polysemous' are sometimes used both for sentences and phrases, and also for words and morphemes taken as isolated elements, or studied as members of a grammatical paradigm[4]. Terminologically this is unfortunate, nor is it merely a matter of terminology. If the

---

[4] For footnote, see next page.

term 'ambiguous' is used both for sentences that can have more than one interpretation and for segmental elements in the sense of their being able to have more than one function within the same paradigm, the term will eventually be applied also in cases where the potential ambiguity of such an element, let us say an affix in an inflectional language, will never be realized on the level of the constructions in which these elements obligatorily occur.

It is conceivable – and is in fact frequently the case – that an element is 'ambiguous' in the analysis of a particular grammatical category because it could indicate, for instance, 'Nominative Singular' and 'Nominative Plural' in a language where Singular and Plural are on independent grounds assumed to be relevant grammatical categories, but that this element, even on the lowest level of grammatical construction always co-occurs with another element that unambiguously specifies whether the first element indicates 'Singular' or 'Plural'. This is a point where the indiscriminate use of the term 'ambiguous' makes it a dangerous metaphor, as pointed out by Hockett (1966) in a discussion of an article by Pike and Erickson (1964). It seems advisable to restrict the term ambiguous to those cases where multiple meaning is an actual possibility, even if this means that the investigation will eventually move on the borderline between language system and language use.

1.3. Sources of ambiguity

After this outline of what will be understood by the ambiguity of sentences, I turn to the question of what the consequences are for a linguistic description.

Starting once more from a general definition, all ambiguities can be viewed as instances of 'homophony': a sentence is inherently ambiguous when it 'sounds the same' but has 'more than one meaning', as in

(2) The soldiers took the port at night
(3) They kept the car in the garage.

And just as it is the task of a linguistic description to explain that sentences have a meaning, so it is also its task to explain the fact that some sentences have more than one meaning.

The definition above, however, is very unspecific, since it is not at all clear what 'sounding the same' and 'having more than one meaning' means. I will therefore assume – begging some important questions, some of which will be

---

[4] For instance Katz and Fodor (1964:497): 'A lexical item whose dictionary entry contains polyadic branching has more than one sense, i.e., is ambiguous'. Ullmann (1962: 156 ff.) uses the term for affixes as well as for sentences, and Quine (1964[2]: 129 ff.) speaks of ambiguity of 'terms' alongside ambiguity of 'expressions'.

discussed later — that a linguistic description involves three levels of representation and their mutual interrelations: a level of phonological representation, a level of grammatical representation and a level of lexical representation. A phonological representation, furthermore, will be assumed — again, for the moment without qualifications — to be equivalent to a representation of formally distinct elements, words and morphemes, and may for practical purposes be replaced by an orthographic representation. We can then say that a sentence is inherently ambiguous when it is 'same' on the level of phonological representation, but 'different' (i) on the level of grammatical representation, as is the case in (3) above where *in the garage* is a complement to *They kept the car* or to *the car* alone and there are two corresponding meanings though the words are identical in both cases, or (ii) on the level of lexical representation only, as is the case in (2) where there are two meanings though the grammatical structure is identical.

From this, it follows that the question of whether or not a sentence is inherently ambiguous is one to be answered from the linguistic description as a whole, and that when we speak of 'grammatical' or 'lexical' ambiguity, what is actually meant is 'non-sameness' within one particular grammatical or lexical description. The problem is then shifted to the question of when it is appropriate and when not to decide that a sentence is 'non-same' in these respects, and this rather controversial issue will concern us in the following chapters. We will then also see that inherent ambiguity is not restricted to the clear-cut cases of homonymy as referred to above that can be described in terms of 'same' and 'non-same'. In a sentence like

(4) The bank was the guerillas' target

the bank can be interpreted as 'some particular financial institution', or as 'some particular building', or it can stand for 'the financial power of society', and *target* can accordingly have different interpretations. Neither *bank* nor *target*, however, are therefore to be viewed as homonymous elements.

A few remarks have to be added on the status of 'phonological representation'. The examples of inherently ambiguous sentences used so far are all conveniently 'same' on the level of morphemic representation. There are other examples, as for instance the French phrases

(5) Celui qui l'aime
    ('The one who loves him, or her, or it')

and

(6) Celui qu'il aime
   ('The one he loves')

that are different syntactically *and* morphemically in the rather unusual way
that the 'same' segmental elements can form more than one morphemic sequence with a grammatical structure. Many of such examples are to be found
in Bally 1944[2]:334 ff., and have become well known more recently in discussions of 'juncture'.

In view of the rather crude distinction of levels made above, such examples
raise the problem of whether they are 'same' on the level of phonological representation, since the 'same' segments are involved, and 'different' only on
the level of grammatical representation and lexical representation, or whether
they are also 'different' on the level of phonological representation, since the
sequential organization into morphemes and words is phonologically marked;
or, whether the phonological segments viewed upon as 'same' are not 'same'
after all, for the linguistic description or for the native speaker.

There is an understandable reluctance to view such constructions as gen-
uine cases of ambiguity, because of the fact that the meanings of many of
them are so far apart that their potential ambiguity will almost immediately
be resolved in actual use, except maybe when one is made aware of the ambiguity in rather elaborate forms of punning. Whether this is true or not –
and it probably is –, these cases cannot be overlooked in a linguistic description of ambiguity. Firstly, because they serve to remind one that many discussions of ambiguity only start *after* one possible source of ambiguity has
been eliminated, viz. after sentences have been unambiguously transcribed
morphemically as in (5) and (6). In the vast majority of cases, this means an
orthographically unambiguous transcription as well; and orthographic conventions may serve to solve various kinds of potential ambiguities, as illustrated
by Bally (o.c. 262) with the French phrases

(7) S'intéresser au grec
   ('To be interested in Greek')
(8) S'intéresser au Grec
   ('To be interested in the Greek')
(9) S'intéresser aux Grecs
   ('To be interested in the Greeks')

Leaving these examples aside, since the problem they pose is different from
the one posed by (5) and (6) above, it can nevertheless be said that many discussions of ambiguity concern themselves mainly with sentences that are
unequivocal as far as the formal identity of their ultimate constituents is con-

cerned. And this, in turn, tends to obscure a second problem connected with the level of phonological representation. It can be disputed — and it has been disputed quite vigorously — whether sentences that *are* unambiguous morphemically, or, that are 'homomorphic' to borrow a term from Pike (1967[2]:574)[5] like

(2) They kept the car in the garage
(10) He hit the man with the stick
(11) They are flying planes

but ambiguous syntactically, are also 'homophonous', or whether they are different on the level of phonological representation as well, by the introduction of prosodic features that correspond with the alternative syntactic representations.

Whatever one's position in this dispute, it will be necessary not to take the level of phonological representation for granted in this respect, even if the only reason was that it raises an important issue, namely the relation between this level and other levels of the description. In the next chapter, I will try to answer some of the questions connected with this.

[5] 'Ambiguous items which have the same morphemes but different tagmemes may be called HOMOMORPHIC.'

2. AMBIGUITY AND PHONOLOGY: LEVELS OF REPRESEN-TATION

2.1. Preliminary remarks

The problem of ambiguity in relation to the level of phonological representation raises different questions.

Firstly, in actual speech, distinguishing features which are assumed to belong to the phonological system of the language, can and often will be absent. In such cases, utterances might therefore be called ambiguous in the sense of 'indistinct' or 'unclear'. This is a problem of linguistic research about which I intend to say very little in this context. It is well known that in general, distortions of various kinds in actual speech will not hinder communication between native speakers. On the other hand, unfinished, ill-pronounced or otherwise semi-acceptable utterances cannot be said to be representative of the language system. They have communicative function by their as yet unclear relation to that language system, to the native speaker's 'knowledge' of it, and possibly also with the help of a variety of other compensatory data. Also, as far as speech sounds in particular are concerned, slurred, rapid, or half audible speech may still be perfectly communicative in many situations.

Partially connected with the above, but more crucial for linguistic description, is the question of which sound features are distinctive in the sense that they contribute to the identification and the distinction of linguistic elements. To reformulate this question in terms of the purpose of this study: to what extent should sentences, or parts of them, that for the native speaker are 'different' grammatically or lexically, also be represented as different on the level of phonological representation? I will assume that this question is at the heart of phonological theory, no matter from what basic assumptions such a theory may start. More specifically, what is involved here is the problem of the interdependence of levels of description on the one hand, and the autonomy of levels on the other hand. The existence of completely 'homophonous' elements like *meet* and *meat*, *can* 'to be able to' and *can* 'tin' is generally recognized, but opinions diverge as soon as the relation between the phonological level and other levels becomes more complicated. This is the case especially when the description of phrases and sentences is concerned, more so than in the description of isolated elements.

11

2.1.1. *'Same' vs. 'different': the post-Bloomfieldian view*

The problem outlined above has come into maximal focus in and due to post-Bloomfieldian phonology. Most descriptions made within this tradition present elaborate analyses of differences in sound, matched by a representation of those differences in the phonological transcription. Moreover, this is usually accompanied by hypotheses and often, firm statements, on 'audibility' as a primary criterion in two respects: as a necessary condition for the application of the 'same or non-same' criterion, and, as a necessary consequence of this criterion once it is adopted. The pivot principle is briefly, and unambiguously, stated in Hockett 1958: 'Sounds and differences between them have one and only one function in language: to keep utterances apart' (p. 15).

Evidently then, if the identity or non-identity of linguistic 'forms' in the Bloomfieldian terminology, is primarily a question of 'sounding the same' or 'not sounding the same', sound is the first criterion upon which this decision is to be made. And as a consequence — at least in practice — those linguistic forms that are 'different' on some higher level, should preferably be 'different' also on the sound level. On the other hand, what counts as 'different' on the sound level, or what counts as a phonemic distinction in one case, in turn determines 'sameness' or 'non-sameness' in other cases, for the sake of consistency in description.

Two 'classic' papers in the Bloomfieldian tradition may serve to illustrate these respective points.

The first is Moulton's description of the segmental phonemes of German (Moulton 1947). On the basis of a first examination based on monosyllabic forms, the velar fricatives [x] and [ç] are described as being in complementary distribution in standard German. Later, in the course of the discussion of the 'open juncture' phoneme /+/, Moulton revises this statement. The words [ku:xen], 'cake' and [ku:çen], 'little cow' are manifestations of a meaningful contrast of [x] and [ç]; this can be accounted for in terms of segmental phonemes by transcribing the two words as /ku:xen/ and /ku:+xen/ respectively. That is, /x/ is [x] after central vowels and back vowels and semi-vowels, but /x/ is [ç] after all other phonemes, including /+/. In /ku:+xen/ 'little cow', the open juncture phoneme /+/ has a zero allophone, or, in free variation, a brief pause. The possibility to regard [x] and [ç] as two different phonemes, is rejected because it conflicts with the original tentative analysis of segmental phonemes.

Whatever may be said about the final solution, it is not an exaggeration to see in it an attempt at reflecting all contrasts that might be meaningful on one and the same level of phonological representation. Also, it is remarkable, but quite consistent with the principles of the description, that the possibility of regarding this 'minimal pair' as grammatically determined rather than by a difference in segmental phonemes is also rejected[1].

An example of the second consequence of the post-Bloomfieldian view — let us call it the 'reinforcement principle' — is Bloch's well-known discussion of phonemic overlapping (Bloch 1941). The argument runs as follows: the difference in length of the vowels of the American English words *bit/bid, bet/bed, pot/pod,* is described as an automatic alternation, viz. compulsory lengthening of vowels before a voiced consonant in word-final position. The difference in vowel length in some American dialects, between the words *bomb/balm,* also present in such pairs as *sorry/starry, bother/father,* is described as phonemic and non-automatic.

Phonetically, the vowel of *bomb* is the same as the vowel of for instance *pot*; the vowel of *balm* is the same phoneme as the vowel of, for instance, *pa.* This would have the consequence that the vowels of the word *pod* and of the truncated phrase *pa'd* in the sentence *pa'd go if he could* are different phonemes, but that the two vowel segments are phonetically the same. There are two solutions for this predicament: either the vowel phoneme of *pa'd* is taken to be identical to the vowel phoneme of *pot* and *pod*; this would entail that there is also no phonemic difference between, say, *balm* and *bomb*. Or, the vowel phoneme of *pod* is taken to be identical to the vowel phoneme of *pa'd*, but this would entail that the difference between the vowels of *pod* and *pot* is phonemic also, and not automatically determined by context. Both solutions follow readily from these assumptions: if two sounds *a* and *b* are in variation but two similar sounds *c* and *d* are in phonemic contrast, and if *c* turns out to be phonetically identical to *a*, and *b* to *d*, either the phonemic distinction between *c* and *d* disappears, or the phonetic distinction between *a* and *b* receives the status of a phonemic distinction. Bloch suggests that one should choose the latter solution 'to account for all the facts of pronunciation, which is surely the more important requirement' (p. 96). The main point, however, is that this paper illustrates the consequences of relying on sound in deciding what is 'same' and what is 'non-same', and that again, in the comparison of *pod* and *pa'd*, grammatical considerations are excluded[2].

It would not be difficult to come forward with other analyses which in this

---

[1] For a critique, see Leopold (1948:215–6).

[2] For a general criticism of one of the principles underlying this analysis, the 'once a phoneme always a phoneme' principle, see Chomsky (1964:90–1).

respect are quite similar in argumentation. The objective of not a few authors within the post-Bloomfieldian tradition appears to have been: a phonological transcription which represents the utterances of a language unambiguously up to a very high degree, and at the same time, the representation should give a true picture of the actual differences in sound.

Against this view can be brought the argument that these two requirements are quite incompatible. It is, in general, doubtful whether the actual discrimination by native speakers between linguistic 'forms' does not presuppose much more than sound to rely on. But even if this problem is left aside for the sake of the argument one must represent as highly dubious the phonological status of several of the sound features that, within this approach, have been claimed to correlate with differences in 'meaning'. This is especially true of the juncture phoneme, and of the various phonemes of intonation. In general, this problem poses itself most acutely with those features that are closely involved with the grammatical level of the linguistic description, that is, with a structure that is mainly non-segmental.

2.2. Junctures and intonation

By 'junctures' and 'intonation' will be understood here, complexes of sound features that might be involved in the distinction of utterances of the language that otherwise would be identical on the level of representation in phonological segments, and hence might be ascribed phonological status.

To facilitate the discussion, I will start from the following terminological distinction: As 'juncture' will be regarded any manifestation of those features which it has been claimed distinguish utterances that are equivocal as to the division of the sequence into morphemes. For example, in

he's a bee feeder / he's a beaf eater

in American English, or in

je l'apporte / je la porte

in French, where the distinctions might be made by marking the transitions at the grammatically crucial boundaries.

By the term 'intonation' will be meant features of pitch, stress, and duration that have been claimed to distinguish utterances that have an unequivocal representation on the level of morphemes, such as

Vandenburgh reports open forum
He hit the main with the stick

but have alternative grammatical structures. Under the assumption that above-mentioned intonational features serve to distinguish these alternative structures, they can be ascribed 'phonemic' status on the same basis as junctures.

2.2.1. *Junctures*

It is not surprising that within the post-Bloomfieldian framework of linguistic description, one possible distinctive feature of sequences of speech sounds, viz. 'juncture', has been paid much more attention to than had been the case previously. The term does not occur as such in Bloomfield's *Language*, but ever since then has been a common part of phonemic analyses worked out on the basis of principles outlined in that book (rather than on the basis of Bloomfield's own phonological practice). Of course, the analysis of 'junctures' is to be seen as a partial continuation of the previously familiar observations on 'word-boundaries' and 'Grenzsignale' that did not, however, play a central role in for instance Praguean phonology.

Thus, whereas Bloomfield ascribes the difference between the phrases *an aim* and *a name* to a difference in stress (1935:113), Trager and Smith (1951) consider such 'minimal pairs' as *an aim* and *a name, nitrate* and *night rate* as distinguished by a transitional sound feature called a phoneme of internal open juncture. It contrasts with close juncture (normal transition between adjacent phonemes within the same linguistic 'form') and external open juncture (or, a pause; see also Bloch and Trager 1942:47). 'Minimal pairs' of the kind quoted are to be found in various other inventories of the phonemes of American English.

2.2.1.1. *Phonetics*

The first thing to be noted here is that the transcriptions of the various occurrences of a 'juncture' phoneme have been quite heterogeneous from the outset. This can be illustrated for instance with the regularly recurring example of the sequence

light house keeper

which can be 'lighthouse-keeper' (one who tends a lighthouse) or 'light housekeeper' (housekeeper that is light in weight). The example comes from Smith 1956. (Originally, a third minimal contrast was mentioned: *light housekeeper* in the sense of 'one who does light housework'. In order to avoid complications, this third interpretation will be omitted from consideration here.)

Smith regards the difference in sound between these two constructions as a difference in stress:

líght+hôuse+keèper   lighthouse-keeper
lìght+hóuse+kêêper   light housekeeper

where the diacritical marks ´, `, and ^, indicate 'primary', 'secondary', and
'tertiary' stress, respectively. Junctures are in this analysis assumed to be distributed in the same way in both constructions.

Bolinger and Gerstman (1957) assume, with other authors, that the transition is not merely or even primarily indicated by a difference in stress levels.
From the results of an experiment, which involved among other things the
artificial alteration of the transitions between *light* and *house*, they conclude
that for native speakers, the distinctive feature is a feature of 'disjuncture'.
This is described as a relative difference in the way the first two syllable-centers
are separated, by lengthening (in the second case) c.q. shortening (in the first
case) of the intervals between the syllables. Schematically, this may be indicated as

light/ house// keeper
light// house/ keeper

A similar conclusion is reached in Lieberman 1967, who, on the basis of an
acoustic-articulatory analysis, equally maintains that the intervals between the
vowels indicate the difference in structure rather than phonetic cues which
should correlate with stress differences. The doubts expressed by Bolinger
and Gerstman, in their article, about the phonetic correlates of the stress levels
usually assigned to such constructions also seem to be confirmed by an experiment reported in Lieberman 1965. Finally, it should be added that according
to Bolinger and Gerstman the natural conclusion is that the disjuncture phenomenon, though acoustically attestable, is not autonomous, but is a function
of the difference in what they call the 'semantic bond' between the constituents in the alternative interpretations of the sequences.

The correlation between stress levels and occurrences of juncture is again
emphasized in Hockett 1958 (54–61), but Haugen (1956) claims that presence
or absence of junctures is to a large extent determined by the nature of syllabification.

A third parameter often mentioned is length. For French minimal pairs
such as *celui qu'il aime* vs. *celui qui l'aime, il a dit* vs. *il l'a dit*, Malmberg
(1944, 1964) assumes that in the second example of each pair occurs a distinctive feature of consonant gemination ([l] vs. [l:]). The difference between implosive vs. explosive realization of the consonants at the boundary,
by other authors regarded as the distinctive feature, according to him is too
weak in French to carry the information. In a semi-minimal pair such as *grand*

dadais vs. *grande Adèle* vowel lengthening possibly also plays a rôle ([grã] vs. [grã:]). Malmberg also points to the relation between occurrences of juncture and the phonetic effects of syllabification. Vowel lengthening is assumed to be distinctive in British English by Sharp (1960) who also introduces the parameter of sentence rhythm and points out that quite complex semantic phenomena may play a considerable rôle as well. Hoard (1966) assumes that for such constructions as

a nice man / an iceman

the primary difference is absence vs. presence of consonant gemination rather than differences of stress or vowel length. And he also maintains that junctures cannot profitably be described without taking into account syllable-formation rules.

I will not go on listing the various types of phonetic features that have been mentioned in the literature, the more so since a comprehensive survey of the phonetic characteristics of internal open juncture is to be found in a report by Lehiste (1960). The aim of her study was to find the acoustic parameters of this type of juncture. With this end in view, phrases spoken both in and out of sentence context were spectrographically analyzed in various ways. Moreover, a listening experiment was done with 25 minimal pairs familiar from current literature, and an extensive and critical survey of previous treatments of juncture, phonetically and phonologically, is presented as well.

The acoustic cues of internal open juncture turn out to be a composite function of various phonetic effects, that together give the impression of a 'bounded sequence'. They can be divided into prosodic features of that bounded sequence itself, such as duration and intensity, and segmental features of allophonic variation at the boundaries between two bounded sequences. For a pair such as

a nice man / an iceman

the main parameters are: length of the consonant /n/, and a difference between the formants of the first segment of the diphthong /ay/. Secondary parameters are: higher intensity of the /n/ when it is initial and a slight glottal catch when it is final. For the majority of the minimal pairs investigated, similar complex differences in phonetic realization could be attested.

The first conclusion, then, is that there is no consistent correlation at all between some particular feature and the occurrence of a juncture, but that its phonetic signalling is heavily dependent on other features of the sequence, and thus may vary from case to case.

The second conclusion Lehiste draws, however, is that the demarcation of
a 'bounded sequence' in connected speech is a relatively autonomous phenomenon, in the sense that it may very well not coincide at all with the grammatical boundaries of the linguistic description. For instance, word boundaries
appear to be marked far more consistently than morpheme boundaries, but internal open juncture may also occur in sequences that grammatically are two
words, etc.

Taken together, the results of the study give an explanation of the variety
of opinions on the phonetic correlates of internal open juncture one comes
across in the literature, including the different ways in which the same 'minimal pair' is sometimes described by different linguists. Both can be viewed as
a reflection of the fact that the actual phonetic correlates of juncture have a
very weak relation to any of the discrete features in the usual phonemic transcriptions.

2.2.1.2. Phonemics

In view of the complex interrelation of the features that can be involved in
the marking of grammatically relevant boundaries, and in view of their relatively high degree of contingency, it is quite understandable that there has
been equally little agreement over the *phonological* status of junctures.
Roughly speaking, opinions range from 'segmental phonemes in their own
right' (e.g. in Moulton 1947, see above p. 12), via 'suprasegmental phonemes'
(for all those who consider junctures mainly as correlated with stress levels) to
'phonetic signalling of morphological and syntactic structure which, though a
feature of sound, is therefore not in itself phonological'. The latter is the conclusion drawn for instance by Lehiste, and by Hoard. In tendency, it is quite
similar to Pike's view, where he speaks of 'emic features of contrast that
should not themselves be regarded as [phon]emes' (1967^2:405). Comparing
these viewpoints with each other, it would appear that the experimental data
point to Pike's conclusion.

It is important to notice, in this connection, that the theoretically delicate
position of junctures as primitives of phonological representation, has not
escaped the notice of post-Bloomfieldian theoreticians. For instance, in an
article by Bernard Bloch (1948:41) the possibility is considered that junctures
will have to be regarded as 'fictions', introduced into the phonemic representation to account for a meaningful contrast[3]. This would imply, first of all,
that 'juncture', if it is viewed upon as a phoneme, ranges over a variety of
'allophones' that form a very heterogeneous set, in fact, a set which is a pho-

---

[3] See also Harris (1963^6: 79–89).

nological set only by definition. It is in particular due to this view that one of
the allophones of open juncture can be 'zero', as is indeed the case in Moulton's description of [kuːxen] vs. [kuːçen]. This appears to be in conflict,
moreover, with the Bloomfieldian standpoint that phonemes have of necessity
a correlation with something that one can hear, since one of the allophones of
internal open juncture would then be inaudible. Secondly, this view would
imply that in one of its occurrences internal open juncture coincides with
close juncture or normal transition. From this, however, it is distinct by definition, as we saw above. On these grounds, the concept of a 'zero allophone of
internal open juncture' has been severely criticized for its theoretical awkwardness by various authors, e.g. Haas (1957), and Pike (1967[2]:406–7).

2.2.1.3. *Grammar*

It would appear, then, that the phoneme of internal open juncture, assumed
to distinguish sequences of identical segments that morphologically or syntactically are distinct, has been introduced mainly on the basis of considerations
that involve these other levels of the description. This is in conflict with the
post-Bloomfieldian axiom that considerations of other levels should *not* enter
into the principles and practice of phonemic investigation and representation.

The viewpoint that the above conclusion is nevertheless unavoidable, and
also the only realistic one, has been carried through consistently in the article
on accent and juncture by Chomsky, Halle, and Lukoff (1956), where the
lighthouse-keeper vs. *light housekeeper* example is taken up once more. The
authors state that, in contrast with the requirements for an analysis and description of true segmental phonemes, junctures will be postulated only for
those cases where phonetic effects can be correlated with a morpheme boundary. This is done in order to achieve 'actual simplifications in the transcription' (p. 68). The constructions are first represented as follows.

líght $-_2$ hóuse $-_1$ kéeper
líght $=_1$ hóuse $-_2$ kéeper

where = is 'external juncture', − is 'internal juncture', and the subscripts 1 and
2 indicate the hierarchy of the constituents in the two different phrases. It is
clear that in this way considerations form other levels are introduced into the
phonological representation in a straightforward manner. Nor is it the authors'
aim to conceal this. Cf. also Chomsky (1964:104):

'We must conclude, then, that there is no known method for assigning junctures in terms of phonetic evidence alone (...) It seems unlikely that this difficulty can be remedied, and unless it is, the principle of separation of levels is
entirely untenable'.

The final stress patterns for the two phrases *lighthouse-keeper* and *light housekeeper*, represented as

1 3   2 4
light house keeper

2 1   3 4
light house keeper

are predicted by the junctural symbols and by the subscripts, both being *grammatical* features. They are arrived at by the application of a set of rules that alter the original primary stress symbols of the constituents. In passing, it may be noted that, phonetically, the difference is again assumed to be a difference in stress, as it was in the original description by Smith. But of course, the theoretical assumptions are quite different.

It can also be seen that this procedure foreshadows the introduction of a close relation between phonological representation and the representation of other levels of description in later transformational publications, and also the final and principal separation of the level of 'systematic phonetics' and the level of 'systematic phonemics' (see especially Chomsky 1964). In fact, the principles outlined in the aforementioned article have been applied, together with the concept of underlying phonological form, for the generation of a substantial part of English derivational morphology in Chomsky and Halle (1968). Also Lieberman, in his recent monograph on intonation (1967), for his description of junctures essentially follows the principles laid out in Chomsky, Halle, and Lukoff (1956): 'The stress levels (assigned to the vowels of a word or a phrase) are a function of the phonemic structure of the word, its syntactic function (e.g. whether it is a noun or a verb in the derived phrase-marker) and the constituent structure of the derived phrase-marker' (149 ff.) He agrees, however, with the Bolinger-Gerstman analysis inasfar as he concludes from his experimental measurements that 'disjuncture' is an acoustic cue.

2.2.1.4. *Junctures and traditional phonology*

Whether one accepts the Transformational view on juncture in its entirety, is another matter, to which I will return. For the moment, some doubts seem all too justified with regard to the 'phonological' status of junctures as distinctive features of sound. In itself, it is possible that grammatical boundaries can be signalled by contrastive sound features, and it is not my purpose to deny this. But the step towards the assumption that junctures are distinctive and therefore primitive elements of a phonological representation – in its traditional sense – is quite a large one to take, and involves some problems that I will try to summarize below.

(i) An investigation of the supposed distinctiveness of junctures will often include an investigation of actual speech, to corroborate the claim that these sound features are distinctive. The manner in which such tests are carried out appears to influence their results in a quite crucial manner, however. This may be seen from a comparison of the experiments reported in Lehiste (1960) and those done by O'Connor and Tooley (1964) for speakers of English. In the first test, 25 'minimal pairs' which were found to be distinct phonetically in the speech of the majority of the test-persons, were played to two groups of listeners. The majority of the original phrases (21 out of 25) were correctly identified by the majority of them. The phrases, however, were presented in isolation, which in my opinion makes the test artificial inasfar as it is meant to be an investigation of distinctiveness. A similar test devised by O'Connor and Tooley, during which the phrases concerned were presented in sentence-context, led to a correct identification of only 34% according to their calculations.

(ii) As we saw earlier, the phonetic correlates of internal open juncture are closely tied up with the phonetic properties of the words and phrases where the grammatical boundaries occur. Hockett (1958) for instance, notes that the stress system and syllable structure of American English does not allow an occurrence of internal open juncture in such phrases as *get a board* as opposed to *get aboard*. In both phrases, the unaccented *a* is not separated from *board*. The acoustic analysis made by Lehiste of these two phrases points to the same conclusion. In connected speech, the phrase *a board* and the word *aboard* are both one bounded sequence of an allophone of /ə/, followed by an initial allophone of /b/. Only when the phrase *a board* is spoken in isolation, does the possibility of a contrast arise, namely when it is emphatically realized as [eɪbɔːrd], where [eɪ] is a sequence of its own.

In their investigation of minimal pairs of the type *grade A* vs. *grey day*, O'Connor and Tooley found that the occurrence of a manifestation of juncture is, to a considerable extent, 'determined by the nature of the consonant occurring at the crux' (1964:176). The highest score of correct identification was obtained at sequences with a Voiceless Stop at the crucial point: *great ape* vs. *gray tape*. This is in accordance with the relatively higher intensity of Voiceless or Tense Stops over and against Voiced or Lax ones in general. In other words, whether a sequence of elements is grammatically interpreted as /——VC # V——/ or as /——V # CV——/ is at least partially determined by factors that in themselves are independent of grammatical structure. This would mean that the occurrences of juncture are subject to the possibilities of the over-all sound system of the language, which in fact is a most natural conclusion. This conclusion stands, even if it entails that there may be no attestable junctures at all where there should be, or that they may occur where, grammatically speaking, there should not be any.

To take an example form Dutch, it is quite possible — at least for my speech — that the sequence of the two words *veer*, /ʃer/, 'ferry' and *over*, /ovər/, 'over' in the sentence

(1) Daar gaat een veer over
      ('There is a ferry crossing there', lit. *'There goes a ferry over')

is distinct from the sequence *veerover*, /ʃé# ròvər/, 'cattle thief', in the sentence

(2) Daar gaat een veerover
      ('There goes a cattle thief')

The final accentuation of the first and of the second sequence will be identical, with a primary accent on the first and a secondary accent on the second syllable. But normally, Dutch /e/ is relatively close before syllable final /r/ but not before syllable-initial /r/[4]. Thus, we have [ʃéròvər] in (1) and [ʃéròvər] in (2). A comparable difference can be attested between the /e/ in *meer*, /mer/, 'more' and the /e/ in *meerijden*, /mé# reιden/, 'to ride along'.

In other cases, however, such signalling of the grammatical boundary is absent. Compare the sequence of the two words *stroop*, /strop/, 'syrup' and *op*, /ɔp/, 'on' in the sentence

(3) Daar zit de stroop op
      ('The syrup is on that one', lit. *'There is the syrup on')

and the sequence *stropop*, /stró# pòp/, 'straw-doll' in the sentence

(4) Daar zit de stropop
      ('There is the straw-doll')

As in the foregoing examples, the final accentuation of the two sequences will be identical. The difference in segmentation, furthermore, is overridden by a quite general rule of syllabification in Dutch which says that the word-final consonant of /strop/ in (3), in that position is undistinguishable form the initial consonant of /pɔp/ in (4). The /o/ is affected in neither case, and both sequences will sound as [strópɔ̂p]. Cf. the sequences *loop op*, [lópɔ̂p] and *koop op*, [kópɔ̂p] in the sentences

---

[4] This, of course, is already a simplification. Actually, both [e] sounds will be influenced by the following [r], but in *meerijden* the [e] will be affected to a degree that is sufficiently low for its interpretation as syllable-final.

(5) Ik loop op straat
   ('I walk on the street')
(6) Ik koop op bestelling
   ('I buy to order')

It is possible to emphasize the difference in grammatical structure of the sequences in (3) and (4) in very careful speech, but in normal conversational style, the difference will have no phonetic correlates. By the same token the word *koper*, /kop#ər/, 'one who buys' is completely homophonous with the morphologically unstructured word *koper*, /kopər/, 'copper'.

   To investigate all the conditions under which grammatical boundaries in a given language can or cannot be signalled, will of course complicate the final picture considerably. If one wants to maintain any correlation of the juncture phenomenon with sound features at all, however, this is the only course to take. The recognition that there is an asymmetry between the grammatical and the phonological level is then unavoidable.

   In this connection, it is interesting that Lieberman (1967:158) in his investigation of the *lighthouse-keeper/light housekeeper* pair, points out that the presence c.q. absence of 'disjuncture' is only experimentally attested between the elements *light* and *house*, though grammatically it should of course be parallelled with an absence c.q. presence of such a phonetic feature also between the elements *house* and *keeper*.

   (iii) The distinctive rôle of junctures will not only be determined by various features of the sound system of the language, segmental or prosodic, but also by such variables as lexical probability and context, both situational and linguistic. As was again pointed out by O'Connor and Tooley, the correct identification of their minimal pairs was considerably influenced by the relative improbability of one member of the pair as against the other, e.g. *to save Erse* against *to say verse*. One can object that this is irrelevant as long as the investigation is aimed at properties of the sound system and not at variables of actual speech. But since the juncture phoneme is supposed to be a 'distinctive' feature attestable in sound, it seems at least premature not to reckon with those features of speech that could have influence on this distinctiveness.

   In fact, the supposition that such factors play a part, is corroborated by an analysis of the phrase *light heavyweight* carried out by Lieberman. In this sequence, no features of 'disjuncture' comparable to what was found in the analysis of *light housekeeper*, were attested. Lieberman assumes, quite plausibly, that this can be explained by the absence of a 'minimal counterpart' **lightheavy-weight*. On p. 125, he makes the general statement: 'It is only when ambiguity arises, that intonation becomes important.'

A similar remark can be found in Malmberg (1964), who also assumes that the *need* to distinguish will to a considerable extent determine the occurrence of junctures. This may be true in fact, but it does not make the status of junctures as primitives of the description in a traditional phonological framework any the better. It is plausible that a native speaker of Dutch will have no difficulty in identifying the sequence *kop-pijn* (colloquial for 'headache') when it is realized as [kɔpêɪn] without any detectable gemination of the consonant at the morpheme boundary or any other transitional feature. There may, moreover, be two reasons for that: firstly, there is no 'minimal counterpart' *ko-pijn* or a minimal counterpart *kop-ijn*; secondly, the first counterpart, a compound with the morphological structure *ko-pijn* could not even exist, since Lax vowels will not occur in word-final position. Theoretically, however, this latter situation is quite different from the first one. The non-occurrence of a juncture when a minimal counterpart is accidentally lacking, or its occurrence in a case where there is a minimal counterpart and an ambiguity might arise, would make 'junctures' partially dependent on extra-linguistic factors to a degree that will be quite high but rather difficult to evaluate, and quite unfit for phonological representation.

There is a comparable problem with Malmberg's conclusion (1944:63) that even the mere possibility of phonetic signalling of grammatical boundaries is sufficient to ascribe these phonetic features phonological status. Within a traditional phonological framework at least, this, in my opinion, does not follow at all. It is one of the basic principles of such a description that one discriminates between features that are 'distinctive' — and hence 'phonological' —, features that are non-distinctive but under properly defined circumstances could replace the distinctive features, and features that might be present under circumstances that, as we saw, are rather ill-defined linguistically.

In view of the foregoing, some scepticism with regard to the juncture phoneme seems to be in order. Also, it may be viewed as established that the autonomous rôle of sound in post-Bloomfieldian phonology has been unduly emphasized. Once this is recognized, however, there are still different ways to look at this vexed problem.

One view is, that junctures are phonetic features that may mark a relevant transition in a sequence, that may, in particular, correlate with a grammatical boundary. That this seems to be all that can be said for the moment, and that the contribution of such phonetic features to disambiguation in actual speech is to a great extent a secret that will only be solved by a combined effort of linguists, phoneticians, and psychologists, is the view that I would essentially defend here.

Another view, which emerges from Transformational publications on the subject, is that junctures are solely primitives of the grammatical representation. I am not sure whether this view on the relation between grammatical and phonetic representation answers all the questions connected with the juncture problem, though as a model of description in general it is undoubtedly more acceptable than the post-Bloomfieldian model.

2.2.1.5. *The transformational view*

It may be useful to make some remarks here on the general format of transformational phonology, as it has been put forward particularly in Chomsky and Miller (1963), Chomsky (1964), Halle (1964), Chomsky and Halle (1965, 1968). I will concentrate on those features that directly bear on the subject: the relation between phonology and grammar, especially with regard to the representation of linguistic expressions that grammatically are ambiguous.

Schematically, then, the rôle of the phonological component of a Transformational-generative grammar may be pictured as follows. The phonological component is 'interpretative' in the technical sense that its rules operate upon strings of elements generated by the (central) syntactic component. The phonological structure of the elements that form these strings is specified by (abstract) distinctive features, their morphological and syntactic structure by a specification of constituent structure. By the application of rules that are partially cyclically ordered, partially not so ordered, the phonological component eventually produces as its output a phonetic representation. Various provisions have been introduced since the model was presented first, such as a difference between rules that do and rules that do not operate on strings that are words morphologically (Chomsky 1967b), and a separate (sub)component that takes care of intonational features that have to do with emphasis, contrast, or topicalization (Chomsky unpublished). Especially, there should be mentioned in this connection the so-called 'readjustment rules' (Chomsky and Halle 1968), that are to be viewed as operations intermediate between the processes that generate the syntactic surface structure and the application of the rules of the phonological component. They serve to determine the maximum domain of the operation of phonological rules, referred to as the 'phonological phrase'.

Formulated otherwise, the input to the phonological component is a 'systematic phonemic' representation, which is non-ambiguous in the technical sense that every string represented has one and not more than one derived constituent structure. The output of the phonological component is a 'systematic phonetic' representation, somewhat parallel to what is known traditionally as a narrow transcription (Chomsky 1964:69) and thus still above the level of free variation of the gradient variety.

An example from Chomsky (1964:68) is the phrase *telegraphic code*, which is represented on the level of systematic phonemics as

$$[NP[Adj[N[Pre^{tele}][Stem^{græf}]]^{ik}][N^{k\bar{o}d}]]$$

and on the level of systematic phonetics as

$$[t^h eligræ\ fikk^h \overset{3\ 5\ 2\ 4\quad 1}{\partial wd}]$$

Similarly, the words *decided* and *delighted* would be represented (p. 74) on the systematic phonemic level as

    dīsayd#d   dīlayt#d

and on the level of systematic phonetics as

    dīsaˑyDɨd   dīlayDɨd

Details of grammatical structure and of underlying phonological form, for instance of the diphthong /ay/, are left out here; they do not bear on the argument as it was presented, together with these and other examples, in Chomsky (1964). Of course, both the systematic phonemic and systematic phonetic representation should be given in the form of feature matrices of which the orthographic and phonetic symbols are no more than convenient abbreviations.

The point at issue is, that on the level of systematic phonemics the final phoneme of the stem of *decide* is represented as /d/, the final phoneme of the stem of *delight* as /t/. On the level of systematic phonetic representation, both consonants are represented with the so-called 'alveolar flap' [D] typical of the American English pronunciation of these consonants in this position. The difference, on this level, is a difference in length between the first element of the diphthong /ay/.

As is well known, these proposals were originally made in the context of a criticism of traditional or 'taxonomic' phonemic representations (see especially Chomsky 1964:75 ff.). In particular, with respect to the examples *decided* and *delighted*, above, Chomsky argues that an 'autonomous' phonemic representation on a level between 'systematic phonemics' and 'systematic phonetics', where the two words would by some authors be represented as

    dīsayd#d   dīlayt#d

has at its best practical or orthographic significance (Chomsky and Halle 1965:99) but no theoretical significance in the description of natural languages. The 'autonomous' or 'taxonomic' representation on this intermediate level, in other words, is regarded as hybrid. It would on the one hand indicate the morphological difference between the final consonants of *decid-* and *delight-* which is phonetically neutralized, and would on the other hand not indicate on this level of 'broad' transcription the difference between the diphthongs. Moreover, the procedures and theoretical insights on which such a representation is based are regarded as ill-founded.

In contradistinction, Chomsky argues that the model of phonological structure adopted in Transformational grammar is theoretically more justifiable and more fruitful. One of the basic points on which these two views of phonological representation differ is, of course, that information on grammatical structure is present throughout on the level of 'systematic phonemics'. Inasfar as any linguistic description is a hypothesis on the way in which sound is related to meaning, in this model the role of syntax is all-important in this relationship.

It should be added that it is also claimed that this model might possibly be closer to the reality of speech perception. The following quotations from Chomsky and Miller 1963 are relevant here and therefore given quite extensively:

'In order to determine a phonetic representation, the phonological rules must utilize other information outside the phonemic representation; in particular, they must utilize information about its constituent structure. Consequently, it is in general impossible for a linguist (or a child learning the language) to discover the correct phonemic representation without an essential use of syntactic information. Similarly, it would be expected that in general the perceiver of speech should utilize syntactic cues in determining the phonemic representation of a presented utterance — he should, in part, base his identification of the utterance on his partial understanding of it, a conclusion that is not at all paradoxical' (p.314).

'In short, a phonetic output that has an appearance of great complexity and disorder can be generated by systematic cyclic application of a small number of simple transformational rules, where the order of application is determined by what we know, on independent grounds, to be the syntactic structure of the utterance. It seems reasonable, therefore, to assume that rules of this kind underly both the production and perception of actual speech.(...) This suggests a somewhat novel theory of speech perception — that identifying an observed accoustic event as such-and-such a particular phonetic sequence is, in part, a matter of determining its syntactic structure (to this extent, understanding it). A more usual view is that we determine the phonetic and phonemic constitution of an utterance by detecting in the sound wave a

sequence of physical properties, each of which is the defining property of
some particular phoneme; we have already given some indication why this
view (based on the linearity and invariance conditions for phonemic representations) is untenable' (p. 318).

In an evaluation of the Transformational view on the relation between
sound and grammar, both from the standpoint of linguistic description and
from the standpoint of the actual perception of speech[5], it may be noticed,
first of all, that there is a non-negligible difference between Chomsky's earlier
approach to this problem, and the later proposals. It is true that the description of junctures as contained in Chomsky, Halle, and Lukoff, is in principle
no different from the current descriptions such as those found in Chomsky
and Halle (1968). Also, the criticism leveled against 'traditional phonology', in
the sense of post-Bloomfieldian phonemics especially, can already be found
in Chomsky's unpublished study *The logical structure of linguistic theory*
(1955a; see, for instance, chapter V on the 'once a phoneme always a phoneme' principle, mentioned above, p. 13). There is also ample evidence, however, that Chomsky did, at that time, not regard an 'intermediate' level of
phonemic representation as completely dispensable, and that he did not reject the 'traditional' notion of 'distinctness'. In chapter I, it is said that two
utterance tokens U_1 and U_2 are distinct if they do not conform, and that this
conformity, for instance for such pairs as *take the latter* / *take the ladder* will
have to be established by an a-semantic pair test. Furthermore, on the level
of phonemic representation there can be conforming tokens that have different representations on the morphemic level, as for instance /əneym/ for
both *an aim* and *a name*. Non-conforming tokens may have identical representations on the morphemic level: *wife* for /wayf/ and /wayv(z)/. The pair
a name / *an aim* returns in Chomsky (1957:85) 'for many English speakers,
the phoneme sequence /əneym/ can be understood ambiguously as either
'a name' or 'an aim'. If our grammar were a one-level system dealing only with
phonemes we would not have an explanation for this fact'.

I will not go here in the, at the time extensively discussed claim, as to
whether an 'a-semantic operational pair test' could indeed serve to indicate
what is distinct and what is not for native speakers. These matters have hardly
been further pursued in subsequent publications. Similarly, the notion 'distinctness' itself, as it is used in traditional phonology, has been since rejected.
It is sufficient to conclude that in *Syntactic structures* for instance, Chomsky's

---

[5] A generative grammar is not to be equated with a model of the speaker or the
hearer. Since, however, arguments like the ones quoted have been adduced on various
occasions, it would be pointless to ignore them.

opinion of the relation between the phonemic level and other levels of the description was not essentially different from the traditional post-Bloomfieldian standpoint. On p. 58, it is stated that the various problems that arise when morphemes are literally viewed as classes of sequences of phonemes, can be avoided 'by regarding morphology and phonology as two distinct but interdependent levels of representation related in the grammar by morphophonemic rules'. In the current version of Transformational phonology, the two phrases *a name* and *an aim* would receive a different representation on the level of systematic phonemics, and another — possibly, in this case, identical — representation on the level of systematic phonetics, related through various intermediate stages by interpretative rules. The level of 'systematic phonemics', it should be emphasized, does not 'replace' the traditional level of 'morphophonemics', though it may in practice be similar to it in some cases. There is no intermediate stage of representation that is identical to the level of 'autonomous' phonemics, where, for instance, in the post-Bloomfieldian approach, *a name* and *an aim* might be represented as distinct by a segmental phoneme of internal open juncture.

This quite radical change in the position of the level of phonemic representation of sentences and phrases thus has its consequences, especially for those that are 'ambiguous': they will be 'different' — since they are grammatically different — on the level of systematic phonemics, that is, the labelled surface structure generated by the syntactic component. Whether they are finally same or different on the level of systematic phonetics depends on the scope of the interpretative rules of the phonological component.

2.2.1.5.1. *'Same' vs. 'different'*

A main reason for rejecting the traditional level of phonemic representation as insignificant for linguistic description and replacing it by the descriptive model outlined above has been, as said before, the theoretical and procedural awkwardness of traditional phonology. However, whether the transformational approach and the traditional notion of 'sameness', both linguistically and perceptually, are indeed so completely incompatible, remains to be seen.

Consider the by now familiar discussion of the alveolar flap in American English. It is assumed (see e.g. Chomsky 1955b, 1964) that such words as *writer* and *rider* are not phonetically distinguished in most American varieties of English by a different intervocalic consonant, but by lengthening of the preceding vowel. The vowel, in this particular example, the first element of the diphthong /ay/ preceding the alveolar that is morphologically /d/, is longer. In both words, the intervocalic alveolar Obstruent is realized as an alveolar flap, [D]. Thus, we have phonetically rayDɨr   (writer)   ra·yDɨr   (rider)

though morphophonemically in the traditional sense we would have

rayt#r   rayd#r

The phonetic representation is arrived at through two rules (Chomsky 1964: 73–4 and 82 ff.) which may be abbreviated to:

(1) a → a·   in the context — (Glide) Voiced

(2) t,d → D in the context stressed vowel — unstressed vocalic.

Chomsky points out that a phonemic description which is based on some criterion of distinctiveness will on this and an indefinite variety of similar points be forced to draw conclusions that go against its own principles. The difference in sound [-a-] / [-a·-], would, within such a framework, have to be assigned to two different phonemes: since these sounds are in 'meaningful contrast' in the context [-yD], they have phonemic status. This would result in establishing a phonemic contrast short /a/ - half long /a·/, which however in American English, has a very limited distribution and should therefore rather be eliminated (Chomsky 1955a, ch. I; 1964:88). This predicament — compare the discussion by Bloch, p. 13 above — could be avoided by assigning [D] in the first sequence -[rayDɨr]- to the phoneme /t/ and in the second sequence -[ra·yDɨr]- to the phoneme /d/ by some principle of 'rephonemicization' of contextual variants. Such a procedure would, no matter its degree of sophistication, amount to the assignment of a non-contrasting sound -[D]- to two different phonemes, and the assignment of two phonetically contrasting sounds -[a] and [a·]- to the same phoneme. This would violate the cherished requirements of linearity and bi-uniqueness: phonemic differences should be in correspondence with phonetic differences in the same order, and a phonemic difference should correspond consistently to one particular set of phonetic features, and the correspondences should also hold in the reverse direction.

It is undeniable that many of Chomsky's arguments against traditional phonology, and especially against the post-Bloomfieldian version of it, are valid. It is another question whether for a linguistic description that does not want to reject the traditional level of phonological representation completely, such pairs as *writer/rider, latter/ladder, putting/pudding* dó offer an insurmountable obstacle. Some of the problems exposed by Chomsky seem to originate from a rather narrow view on 'minimal pairs' as the basic concept of phonological description, and a strictly segmental or 'paradigmatic' view of phonological analysis.

Suppose that in the analysis of the sounds of American English it is established that the contrast between the Voiced and Voiceless – or perhaps rather Lax and Tense – Obstruents [d] and [t] is relevant in the sense that there are many words that are 'different' only by this contrast, in word-initial, word-medial and word-final position. In certain phonetically and sometimes also grammatically definable contexts this contrast is eliminated: in intervocalic position before unstressed vowels. (As a matter of fact, 'neutralization' here has to be understood in the sense that, phonetically, the alveolar flap [D] is voiced rather than voiceless, but that in terms of distinctive features it is neither Voiced nor Voiceless; see also Malécot and Lloyd 1967). In such words as *latter/ladder, writer/rider, putting/pudding,* the only relevant phonetic difference above the level of free variation is a difference in length between the vowels that precede the [D]. This seems to be generally agreed on. Though Householder (1965) claims that the difference could very well reside in other features, for the moment we will take it for granted that the difference is in the vowel. To this it should be added, however, that the example *writer/rider* in Chomsky (1964), which was apparently taken from Harris, is phonetically less fortunate inasfar as Malécot and Lloyd's experimental investigation points to the conclusion that the alleged correlation between difference in Vowel length and Voicing, is *not* experimentally attested in the case of diphthongs, as in *writer/rider* and *fated/faded.* This, however, does not affect Chomsky's argument in principle.

The difference in vowel length in American English is a regular correlate of the difference Voiced/Voiceless or Lax/Tense of the immediately following alveolar stop: *bet/bed, pot/pod.* In view of these data, then, and in view of what is known of the phonetic correlates of the Lax/Tense distinction, it seems not at all unreasonable to ascribe this difference in vowel quality, which in general is not structurally relevant to English words, to some other segment of the word. In particular, to regard this contexually restricted difference in Vowel length as a compensatory feature of the Voiced/Voiceless distinction of the Obstruent that is here neutralized.

Such a solution, of course, depends on various presuppositions. It presupposes, for one thing, that a description of the phonological system of the language does not rely on sound and sound differences only, it presupposes a fortiori that a linguistic description does not proceed from sound to sentence, and it presupposes that a description of the segmental features of a word is only a stage in the analysis, and not its final aim[6].

---

[6] What it does *not* presuppose, *pace* Postal (1968:x ff.; 24 ff.) is that phonology has therewith declared itself to be 'autonomous' in the sense of independent from considerations of higher levels.

In particular, it starts from the assumption that there is a phonological level where sounds pattern 'differently', that are phonetically 'same', and where sounds can be 'same' that are phonetically 'different', if such a solution can be made plausible within the linguistic description. But this, to be sure, has been a commonplace with every phonological description that seeks to discover the structurally relevant features of a language and does not exclusively focus its attention on phonetic 'substance' and distributional procedures.

It may be argued against such an approach, that what it does is in fact admitting grammatical considerations of 'sameness' and 'non-sameness' into the phonological description, without explicitly saying so, and that already for that reason it is theoretically undesirable, and only reinforces Chomsky's arguments. This, however, is not necessarily the case. The phonetic difference in vowel length, ascribed to a phonological difference of the adjacent Obstruent, is found in such morphologically similar pairs as *betting/bedding, fattish/faddish* (examples are from Malécot and Lloyd). It is also to be found in the pairs *latter/ladder* and *putting/pudding*, where the second word of each pair is morphologically unstructured, and in a pair like *atom/Adam*, where both elements are morphologically simplex. The facts are, that a feature of length, co-occurring with the distinction between Voiced and Voiceless in Obstruents, influences the quality of the preceding vowel; and that in some cases, this feature becomes the only feature by which otherwise identical words are 'different', whether or not this corresponds with an underlying grammatical structure. This, of course, puts the isomorphy between such a level of phonological representation and the level of underlying grammatical representation still more in disorder; but that, after all, is not necessarily a shortcoming of the linguistic description.

Nor does such a solution seem to be at variance with the Sapirian concept of the 'psychological reality of phonemes', to which Chomsky has referred more than once in connection both with the linguistic validity and with the perceptual plausibility of his level of systematic phonemics[7]. If the contrast Voiced/Voiceless is relevant in American English stops, on the level of the phonological structure of words, and if the contrast Long/Short is generally not relevant with vowels in *pot/pod, latter/ladder, writing/riding*, it seems quite natural that a native speaker who 'knows' his language in the sense that he 'knows' the phonological system of his language will ascribe the feature

---

[7] See for instance Chomsky (1964:69): 'The level of systematic phonemics is, essentially, the 'phonological orthography' of Sapir (cf. Sapir 1933), his 'ideal sounds' and 'true elements of the phonetic pattern'.' Cf. also Chomsky and Halle (1965, *passim*). A more cautious formulation is to be found in Chomsky and Halle (1968, p. 74–5, fn. 23).

'Long' — or rather, the feature 'relatively Long' — in these words to the Obstruents, in accordance with the pattern he is familiar with. Compare the following quotation from Chomsky and Halle (1965):

'We see nothing strange in the conclusion that perceptual distinctions may be heavily determined by SET and need not correspond in any simple way to physical stimuli (...). In the case of language, the speaker's 'set' is largely a matter of his knowledge of the language, and this may (in fact, surely does) lead him to make perceptual judgements that are not simply related to physical facts (...). Similarly, we see nothing strange about the conclusion that an underlying base form may be 'perceived' (or internally represented in the process of interpreting and utterance) although it corresponds to no identifiable part of the sound stimulus' (p. 136).

Compare also p. 138, fn. 28:

'Many different considerations (...) might lead to the conclusion that segment types must be distinguished phonologically despite the absence of any phonetic contrast between the feature sets'.

One can agree with this view in general without at the same time subscribing to all the implications it might have. From the above quotation, as well as from the context of the discussion it was taken from, emerges the idea that the decision on 'same' or 'non-same' is primarily a matter of *grammatical* 'sameness' or 'non-sameness', and that the perception of the native speaker in such cases should be first and foremost determined by his 'knowledge' of the *grammatical* structure. This is also apparent from the quotations from Chomsky and Miller (1963) given earlier. One might just as well say that such elements as *atom* and *Adam* are different for the native speaker, just as *latter* and *ladder* are, or *betting* and *bedding*, and that in some cases this may correspond to a difference in underlying stem, and in other cases not. What Sapir states in his famous article on the psychological reality of phonemes (1949) is 'that a given phoneme is not sufficiently defined in articulatory or acoustic terms but needs to be fitted into the total system of sound relations peculiar to the language' (p. 46). There is in my opinion no evidence, from this article nor from his 'Sound patterns' (1925) that the reality that Sapir called 'psychological' should be exclusively interpreted in terms of 'the reality of underlying morphological or syntactic structure', though this is clearly the interpretation favoured by Chomsky.

2.2.1.5.2. *Some examples*

To illustrate this point in connection with junctures, I will adduce some examples from Dutch compounding.

Compare the words *schanddaad* 'outrage' and *wandaad* 'misdeed'. The first has an underlying form /sxɑnd#dad/, lit. *shame-act', the second has an underlying form /wɑn#dad/, lit. 'mis-act'. By a rule of assimilation, the two adjacent identical stops in /sxɑnd#dad/ will assimilate to a considerable degree, and in most cases completely, so that we finally have [sxándàt] . This rule is needed also because it reflects a difference in this respect between Dutch stops and Dutch fricatives: two identical fricatives in this position will *not* assimilate completely. It is possible, however, that such differences in morphological structure as between /sxɑnd#dad/ and /wɑn#dad/, will in some cases be marked transitionally. In *schanddaad* for instance, by tensing or lengthening of the stop /d/, possibly accompanied by a lengthening or increased intensity of the preceding /n/: [sxán·t̯àt] . This, however, certainly does not apply to a compound like *handdoek*, 'towel', though grammatically this is /hɑnd#duk/, lit. 'hand-cloth'. In standard pronunciation, the assimilation of the two stops into one is complete here. This can be explained by the fact that for native speakers, *handdoek* is semantically a semi-compound only, and in this respect not comparable to for instance *vingerdoek*, lit. 'finger-cloth'. In any case, there is no appreciable difference between the realization of the /d/ in /hɑnd#duk/ and the /d/ in a word like *zondag*, /zɔn#dɑx/, 'Sunday'.

As another example, consider a compound like *mei-land*, /meɩ # land/, 'May country'. Even if it should perhaps not 'exist', it is a perfectly regular compound. The inherent stress pattern, /méɩ # lànd/, can be assumed to persist, or to be replaced by another marking of the transition between the two constituents. Besides this compound, however, we have a compound such as *weiland*, 'meadow', which morphologically is /wéɩ#lànd/, 'grass-land', but which is pronounced with a marked reduction of the prominence on the second syllable and without any indication of its compositional structure. In this respect, it is completely identical to such words as *eiland*, 'isle' and *heiland*, 'saviour'. Both these two latter words can in the last resort be regarded morphologically as composed of the stem *land* in the first case, /éɩ#lànd/, and from the stem *heil*, 'salvation' in the second case, /héil#ând/. But this difference in underlying structure disappears by force of the syllabification rule mentioned above in the case of *stroop op* vs. *stropop*[8]. And again, it is quite well possible that it is a semantic feature rather than morphological structure that influences the final realization of *weiland, eiland,* and *heiland.*

Another problem may be illustrated with a small section of the formation of Dutch diminutives.

---

[8] Though here the question arises of whether words like *eiland* are to be viewed as compounds at all.

Compare the words *maan*, 'moon' vs. *man* 'man', and *maand*, 'month' vs. *mand* 'bucket'. In underlying form they may be represented as /man/ vs. /mɑn/ and /mand/ vs. /mɑnd/. A quite general rule – though its application is not at all clear in other cases – says that after the addition of the diminutive suffix *-tje*, /tjə/, or maybe just /tj/, a schwa is inserted after Nasals preceded by a Lax vowel, but not after Nasals preceded by a Tense vowel. Thus, for the first pair of words, we finally have *maantje*, [mañt∫ˌə], 'small moon' and *mannetje*, [mɑnət∫ˌə], 'little man'. By another rule, the /t/ of the diminutive suffix is deleted after Obstruents: thus, for the second pair of words, we have *maandje*, [mañt∫ˌə], 'small month' and *mandje*, [mañt∫ˌə], 'small bucket'. The word *mandje*, with palatalization of the /t/ and the preceding /n/, can be readily interpreted since by the rule of schwa-insertion it is distinct from *mannetje*. The final realizations of *maantje* and *maandje*, on the other hand, are completely identical: [mañt∫ˌə].

The number of words, however, where this homophony occurs is very restricted. Normally, vowels are Lax before Nasal plus Dental Stop, and Tense vowels in this position will be interpreted as Substandard or dialectical, e.g. [lant] for [lɑnt], *land*, 'land'. That this is a tendency in the Dutch phonological pattern also appears from the existence of alternative forms with reduced vowels for such words as *vriend*, /vrind/, 'friend' and *eind*, /ɛɪnd/, 'end': *vrind*, /vrɪnd/ and *end*, /end/. This poses the question, as soon as such notions as 'psychological reality' or 'native speakers' intuition' are invoked, of whether the interpretation of a word like *haantje*, /han#tjə/, 'chicken', which has no counterpart **haandje*, /hand#tjə/, is governed by the native speakers' knowledge of the morpheme-structure rule that vowels are Lax before Nasal plus Dental Stop, or by his knowledge of the underlying grammatical structure of the individual word. And it is clear that in the case of [mant∫ˌə], above, no phonetic cues are available to determine the underlying structure.

When 'junctures' are viewed as grammatical elements, they will have a reflection when that is predictable by regular rules – as in the case of the difference between *mandje* and *mannetje* – and they will have no reflection if the same rules predict the non-occurrence of a phonetic realization, as is the case with *maantje* and *maandje*. Though the discussion by Chomsky and Halle of these matters is tentative (see 1968:24–6, 364–73; also p. 5, fn. 1), it appears that no other boundaries, except maybe optional word-boundaries will appear in systematic phonetic representation. This leaves the somewhat more intermediate cases, where phonetic junctures are not predictable by underlying structure only, but which might be explainable by lower level rules of phonetic structuring, involving less general conditions of assimilation, syllabification, and stress reduction, and various semantic factors as well. In this connection, it should be noted that Chomsky and Halle reject the notion of the syllable, though it is doubtful whether the syllable can be dispensed with in a complete description of systematic phonetics.

Summarizing, the Transformational view on junctures, in its criticisms of the post-Bloomfieldian approach, and combined with its general emphasis on the priority of underlying structure, can easily lead to an exaggeration on the other side. Firstly, words or phrases may be assumed to be 'different' for native speakers simply because they are different in underlying form[9], secondly, the problem of those phonetic junctures that can only partially be explained by underlying regularities becomes somewhat more of a pseudo-issue than is defensible.

It should be added, however, that this difference of opinion on the description of junctures is a matter of degree rather than of principle. Also, it should be emphasized in this context that Chomsky never defended the view that phonological structure is wholy *determined* by syntactic structure (see Chomsky 1964:105–6) whereas it cannot be denied that in the post-Bloomfieldian model the view *has* been defended that phonemic representations which account for all meaningful contrasts should be arrived at independently of other levels.

2.2.1.5.3. *Interpretation*
Nor does the transformational model of description give all the answers to the problem raised by the fact that features such as juncture are by all evidence closely tied up with such factors as lexical probability, the context, and the speech situation in general.

It has been demonstrated quite convincingly by Lieberman (see above, p. 20) that the acoustic feature of disjuncture may be used to disambiguate the constituent structure (p. 146), though, as remarked, this would make the occurrence of junctures contingent on a variety of factors.

The important rôle of underlying structure both in the realization and the perception of such phrases is also illustrated by Lieberman with another test. The sequence

     light house keeper

---

[9] This, in principle, becomes a possibility if one assumes (see above, p. 33) that in some cases 'segment types must be distinguished phonologically despite the absence of any phonetic contrast between the feature sets'. It is, in my opinion, self-evident that such a principle can only be applied with caution.

was taken from the sentence

(7) formerly the life of a lighthouse-keeper was very lonely

where it had been spoken with the appropriate stress levels and features of
disjuncture found to be typical for the grammatical structure *lighthouse-
keeper*. It was inserted into the blank in the recording of the sentence

(8) our maid weighs 180 pounds, but the Joneses have had a — for more
    than fifty years.

Despite the fact that the acoustic properties of the inserted phrase were those
of the structure *lighthouse-keeper*, it was invariably interpreted by listeners as
light housekeeper. According to Lieberman, this experiment underscores once
more the determining rôle of grammatical structure over and against phonetic
data.

On realization, however, it would appear that such a test proves very little
for the problem of the relation between levels of description and for the
problem of speech perception. It proves, that contextual features may override
phonetic features to the extent that a grammatical interpretation is arrived at
which, strictly speaking, is at variance with the phonetic data. This is not
surprising or novel, but does not answer the question as to what extent a linguistic description is allowed to introduce grammatical differences into the
phonological representation. As for speech perception, or interpretation in
general, the conclusion is that the junctures in this case were completely determined for the native speaker by the grammatical structure that in turn is,
as appears from the example, determined by the lexical context, though the
phonetic cues were contradictory. This, again, is quite convincing, but is
hardly a conclusion that can be generalized. That would theoretically have
the consequence that 'disambiguation' on the basis of underlying structure
will take place *if* and only if there is a sentence context that suggests which
grammatical relations are present. In those cases where the sentence context in
which the sequence is embedded still does not give the cues, for instance in the
sentence

(9) he has the most un-heard of job of bee feeder / beaf eater

the sequence will never be disambiguated since there is no context to infer the
grammatical structure from. Formulated otherwise, in (8) the disambiguation
would always be a matter of 'competence', in (9) it would always be a matter
of performance, if it occurs at all. This to me seems to be somewhat unrealistic,
but it would follow from the premises. It is much more plausible, as far as
actual speech is concerned, to assume that 'disambiguation' is *always* a matter

of computing the probabilities over and against the phonetic cues; that in
some cases the phonetic cues are more readily available than in other cases;
and that in some cases they are less necessary than in other cases, whether
they are available or not.

2.2.1.6. *Conclusion*

The question we started from was that of to what extent should a linguistic expression that is or contains a sequence that can be alternatively represented morphemically, also be represented as 'different' on the phonological
level. In fact this question falls into two parts: (i) what is the relation in a linguistic description between grammatical and phonological representation, and
(ii) to what extent will junctural phonetic phenomena contribute to disambiguation in actual speech. The answer to the first question is certainly not
identical to the answer to the second question, since the factors that may actually influence or determine interpretation are partially factors of language
use that cannot easily be incorporated into the principles of a linguistic description.

For both questions, however, in my opinion it is true that the issue is still
unsettled, though with regard to the rather strong assumptions of the post-
Bloomfieldian model some issues at least seem to have been clarified. For the
purpose of this book, I will assume that in any language there is a random
number of the kind of utterances discussed here, that on the level of phonological representation, remain ambiguous, and that there is no reason to assume
that they will be consistently 'disambiguated' to any significant degree in
actual speech on the basis of phonetic data only.

2.2.2. *Intonation*

2.2.2.1. *Intonation and syntactic structure*

Quite similar problems, both of principle and of practice, arise in the evaluation of the discriminatory rôle of intonation. In comparison with junctural
phenomena, there is an additional problem, namely that intonation typically
indicates the function of sentences or parts of sentences in a larger discourse.

As in the case of juncture, I will start from the strongest and most straightforward assumption to be made about the grammatical function of intonation.
This is the claim that in sentences like

(1) He hit the man with the stick
(2) Vandenburgh reports open forum
(3) I'll move on Saturday

to which more than one grammatical structure can be assigned, a difference in intonation that resolves the ambiguity corresponds to the differences in parsing.

Let us understand by sentence intonation a configuration of features of pitch, stress, and length with a certain delimitative function. As the most characteristic feature of sentence intonation I will regard here a contour of differences in pitch and prominence. This contour is partially composed of the inherent accentuation of the elements in the sentence, the accentuation of the larger prosodic units they form, for instance word groups, and their position relative to each other in the sequence, and partially of the pitch pattern that is typical for the language under consideration. Investigations such as that carried out by Cohen and 't Hart (1967) point to the conclusion that at least a majority of sentences of a particular language display a configuration of pitch movements that can be considered as typical, though there will be variations according to the structure of individual sentences.

Let us furthermore disregard so-called 'emotional' or other 'personal' components of intonation, and for the moment restrict ourselves to so-called 'declarative' sentences. I will assume that such sentences, in languages like Dutch, are identifiable by a marked decline of the pitch movement towards the end (and not necessarily by a fall that coincides with its final element; see Cohen and 't Hart o.c. p. 190).

The terms 'stress', 'pitch', and 'length' are used here in the way in which they are commonly understood in the linguistic literature, and no specific claims will be made as to their actual phonetic – acoustic or articulatory – correlates. In particular, I will not go into the problem that most features of 'prominence' that for native speakers are crucial in the perception of so-called stress levels, have to do with 'pitch', that is, frequency, rather than with 'loudness', that is, amplitude. Experimentally this has been established beyond reasonable doubt (see for instance Bolinger 1958; Lieberman 1967; and already Mol and Uhlenbeck 1956). Also, I will ignore the problem that acoustically quite different features may serve to indicate the same functional difference, for instance the fact that a certain 'prominence' does not necessarily correspond with a rise in pitch but can equally well be indicated by a marked fall in pitch contour (some experiments on this are reported in Bolinger 1958).

It will be understood that there is definitely no one-to-one correspondence between grammatical structure and features of intonation. First of all, there are sentences that grammatically are no less ambiguous than the ones quoted above, but where the structure of the sequence does not allow the occurrence of an intonational contour that would resolve the ambiguity by indicating the one structure over as against the other. Under normal circumstances there will, for instance, be no intonational contour to indicate whether the sentence

(4) the shooting of the hunters was terrible

is meant as 'their shooting' or 'their being shot'. One condition for the occurrence of a grammatically relevant difference in intonation is that the structure of the sequence of elements in the sentence, both with respect to inherent
accentuation and with respect to relative position, is such that the difference
in grammatical structure can be indicated. In general, the condition appears to
be that the difference in grammatical structure can be related to a difference
in constituent structure in such a way that this difference corresponds to a
difference in sequential organization. This is the case in the examples (1) to
(3) above, where we have alternative organization of the sequence which can
be roughly indicated by putting bars at the crucial boundaries in the transcription:

(1a) He hit the man/ with the stick
(1b) He hit/ the man with the stick

(2a) Vandenburgh reports/ open forum
(2b) Vandenburgh/ reports open forum

(3a) I'll move on/ Saturday
(3b) I'll move/ on Saturday

It is clearly not the case in (4) or similarly ambiguous 'genitive' constructions,
since the grammatical ambiguity does not correspond to a difference in constituent structure as for instance

(4a) The shooting/ of the hunters
vs.
(4b) *The shooting of/ the hunters

   Secondly, not all ambiguities of scope in terms of constituent structure can
be indicated by intonation. In the Dutch example

(5) Hij zag een man op straat
    ('He saw a man in the street')

the prepositional phrase *op straat* can either be related to *een man* ('a man
who walked in the street') or to *Hij* ('when walking in the street he saw a man').
In the 'neutral' case the intonational contour of such a sentence will be something like

   Hij zàg een mán op stràat

where indicates 'highest prominence' and ` indicates 'second highest prominence', and the unbroken line with a downward slant at the end indicates the declarative intonational contour[10]. There is no way here to indicate the alternative 'scope' of the constituent *op straat* in terms of this intonational contour.

'Neutral' intonation, of course, is a somewhat artificial term, since it may well be doubted whether there is one and only one typical intonation for declarative sentences. Let us understand therefore by 'neutral' intonation, one of the various possible intonational contours which reflects both the sequential structure and the inherent pitch pattern of the sentence, and which is not interpreted by native speakers as 'emphatic', 'contrastive', or otherwise stylistically marked. For the purposes of an evaluation of the grammatical rôle of intonation, this appears to be a legitimate abstraction, though of course it is an abstraction.

Thirdly, even in those cases where constituent structure could be indicated unambiguously by an intonational contour, it is not imperative that such a contour occur. The Dutch phrase

(6) Een brochure over de toekomst van de Universiteit

can mean 'A brochure on the future, (published) *by* the University' or 'A brochure on the future *of* the University', but it can safely be assumed that these and similar cases of ambiguity of scope in actual speech will go entirely unnoticed and unmarked. Moreover, the selection of the one interpretation or the other interpretation by a different distribution of prominence, by native speakers will soon be interpreted as 'emphatic' or 'contrastive' and not as 'neutral' in the sense described above[11]. This supports the conclusion that in many cases the perception by native speakers of grammatically contrasting intonational contours is in fact largely a matter of their knowledge of the grammatical structure. The inherent distribution of the levels of stress or prominence of the elements and their syntactic organization is projected onto the intonational contour rather than interpretation taking place on the basis of actual acoustic signals. With respect to the 'levels' of prominence to be encountered in linguistic transcriptions of intonation patterns, it may be recalled that Lieberman's celebrated investigation of the assignment of stress levels to sentences by linguistically trained observers (Lieberman 1965, see also above p. 16) indicates that such an assignment only defectively corresponds with

---

[10] Ignoring that the pitch pattern will, of course, be interrupted by unvoiced sounds.

[11] Chomsky and Miller (see Lieberman 1967:110) claim that it is impossible for native speakers to make an intonational distinction that would solve the ambiguity of the sentence *flying planes can be dangerous* in isolation.

anything to be substantiated by phonetic analysis. This would appear to be in accordance with the findings reported in Lieberman 1967 that native speakers are in general not able to discriminate between more than two levels of prominence in connected speech (see esp. p. 144 ff.).

This brings us to a point that has already been discussed in connection with juncture in the foregoing section, and need not be repeated extensively. The assignment of degrees of prominence, normally called 'stress' to linguistic elements in a sequence, on the basis of their inherent morphological structure and of the grammatical structure of larger units, is one thing, the actual occurrence of phonetically attestable prominence is another thing. The strongest assumption a linguistic description can make, viz., that the one can be mapped onto the other without modification, has been demolished sufficiently by experimental analysis, though this does not mean that such experiments have solved the problem.

2.2.2.2. *Emphasis and contrast*

As remarked from the outset, one problem of the function of intonation is that the features that are assumed to be typical for an intonational contour are, by definition, related to features that have a less clear relation to grammatical structure. This means that an intonational contour may carry information that is not syntactic or morphological, and that such features may obscure the grammatical function of intonation, even when such parameters as 'register', style of speech, rate of speaking, and emotional composure are left out of consideration.

For instance, it has long been observed (see again Bolinger 1961a) that in English and other languages, so-called 'emphatic' stress and so-called 'contrastive' stress are often mutually undistinguishable phonetically, though semantically they can have a function that for native speakers is different.

Let us understand by 'contrastive' intonation the marked increase of prominence on one or more particular elements in a sequence, and describe its semantic function as 'what the speaker means is this and not something else'. For instance, the sentence

(7a) John saw a BIG bear

where the capital letters indicate the contrastive intonation, can be understood as 'It was a *big* bear John saw, not a *small* one'.

Let us understand by 'emphatic' intonation an increase in prominence that indicates that the speaker wants to emphasize what he is saying in general – or maybe, the fact that he is saying something – and not that there are one or more particular elements he wants to set off from something else. In that case, the increase of prominence is not necessarily restricted to one particular sequence; we could for instance have

(7b) JOHN saw a BIG BEAR

to be understood as an expression of surprise, bewilderment, or enthusiasm according to the situation. But since emphasis can also be expressed by an increase of prominence on one element only, one possible emphatic intonation of (7) would coincide with the contrastive intonation (7a). It is possible, as suggested by Bierwisch (1966:153) that there still is a difference inasmuch as in the case of emphatic intonation the whole of the sentence will be spoken on a relatively higher level of prominence.

In many cases, however, emphatic and contrastive stress will tend to fall together, and this will again depend to a considerable degree on the sequential organization of the sequence in terms of its inherent stress pattern. In such cases, intonational contours add ambiguities instead of solving them. For instance, in Bolinger's example (1961a:105)

(8) Why don't you have SUPPER with us?

the relatively high degree of prominence can equally well be interpreted to mean

(8a) 'why don't you come along and have supper with us?'

as

(8b) 'why don't you have supper with us rather than dinner?'

Compare also the non-neutral intonation of a sentence such as (5) above

(5a) hij zag een MAN op straat

that can equally well be interpreted as 'he saw a man, not a woman' as 'what do you think? he saw a man in the street!'.

Such ambiguities will arise quite often in short sentences like Dutch

(9) Hij slaapt ('He is asleep')

where the anaphoric element *hij* will inherently have low prominence and the verb *slaapt* is automatically the center of the intonation in terms of syntactic prominence. The acoustic and articulatory correlates of 'primary' or 'inherent stress' and of emphatic or contrastive stress are, of course, quite similar in nature, since in both cases degrees of frequency, duration, and sound pressure are involved[12]. In non-neutral intonation, such parameters can be raised to a higher degree, but if in a sentence like (9) one wants to stress *slaapt* contrastively or emphatically, in both cases the result will be

(9a) Hij SLAAPT

where emphatic and contrastive stress are, without contextual clues, completely undistinguishable. In fact, one can even doubt to what extent inherent syntactic prominence and non-neutral prominence will be distinguished when, as in (9), the element that gets extra stress is also the element that has inherent stress syntactically, and moreover is marked by the decline of the intonational contour at the end of the sentence.

Again, this does not mean that these different functions of intonation will not be distinguished in a linguistic description. It is well known that native speakers have in general no difficulty in assigning different functions to phenomena that, phonetically, are quite similar in nature. It does mean, however, that, on occasion, such functions may be very hard to discriminate in one particular sentence.

Nor, for that matter, is the 'functional' or 'linguistic' distinction between emphasis and contrast so easy to maintain consistently.

In an unpublished paper by Lu (1965), two different underlying structures are proposed for the sentence

(10) John PLAYED

with marked prominence on *played*. The one structure corresponds to the 'contrastive' interpretation, and is represented as follows

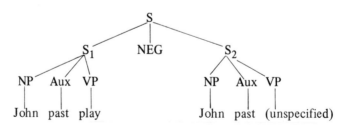

The other structure corresponds to the 'emphatic' interpretation, and is represented as follows:

---

[12] Lieberman (1967:144 ff.).

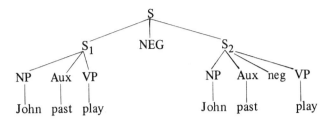

The higher prominence on *played* in the derived constituent structure, in the first case corresponds with the occurrence of a second, unspecified VP of the S_2 in the underlying structure, and in the second case corresponds with the VP *played* preceded by the negation element in the S_2. The rough paraphrase of 'contrastive' and 'emphatic' intonation is then: 'John played and it is not the case that he did do something else' and 'John played and it is not the case that he did not play' respectively.

It would appear that various matters are overlooked in such an analysis. Firstly, there is the question of whether it is at all plausible to connect these intonational differences with syntactically different deep structures. Positing different deep structures in general implies that an ambiguity is regarded as coincidental to the extent that it is explained by assuming more than one underlying structure. For instance, the occurrence of a prepositional phrase like *with the stick* in (1) which is either connected with the Verb or with the Object can be regarded as a coincidental homonymy that can be explained by assuming different deep structures. There are various reasons for doubting whether this is an advisable course to follow here. Firstly, because as we saw the phonetic realizations of emphasis and contrast are markedly similar throughout; secondly, because emphatic and contrastive stress are in point of fact close to each other in their semantic functions also. They are not at all as easily distinguishable as, say, the different interpretations in the standard cases of constructional homonymy. In an utterance like

(11) John was supposed to go to his head of department with his complaints. And what do you think? He went to the PRIME MINISTER!

it is hard to decide whether this is emphatic intonation, or contrastive intonation, even though a context is available.

Furthermore, the paraphrase suggested in Lu's analysis of the 'emphatic' intonation

'John played and it is not the case that he did not play'

is not very satisfactory semantically. It poses the rather awkward problem that since every declarative sentence has a prominence center somewhere, accordingly every declarative sentence might be said to be emphatic, just as every declarative sentence might be said to be contrastive inasmuch as it contrasts with zero, that is, with not saying anything at all.

A third reason to doubt the adequacy of such an analysis is that deep structures assigned to one and the same sentence will pile up endlessly. There are at least four contrastive intonational contours for the Dutch sentence

(12) Hij loopt op straat
('He walks on the street')

including the somewhat uncommon, but quite possible contrast 'he walks ón the street, not únder it'. Explaining these differences by a difference in syntactic deep structure would tend to obscure the fact that these various interpretations of (12) have more in common syntactically than not in common.

From the transformational viewpoint, it seems much more plausible to regard, with Chomsky (unpublished), such features as contrast, emphasis, or topicalization of a particular part of a sentence, as semantic modifications of the same deep structure, and not as disjoint deep structures in their own right[13]. What Chomsky essentially proposes is that the 'intonation center' of a sentence, as for instance *slaapt* in (9) above, determines that part of the sentence that can semantically be regarded as its 'focus' and the other parts, by elimination, as its 'presuppositions'. In sentences like (9) we then would have

(9) Hij slaápt
('He is asleep'), assertion.
(9b) Hij SLAAPT
('I thought he was réading')
(9c) Hij SLAAPT
('To my surprise')

As a further illustration of this point, consider a question like

(13) Liep Jan op het grasveld?
('Did John walk on the grass?')

where *op het grasveld*, 'on the grass', is the intonation center. If this phrase is the focus of the question, it can be answered for instance with

---

[13] Not to mention the problem that elements of a sentence can be topicalized to which no constituent in the underlying phrase marker corresponds (see Chomsky o.c.).

(14a) Nee, hij zat thuis
  ('No, he was at home')

or with

(14b) Nee, hij liep op het voetpad
  ('No, he walked on the foothpath')

but also with just

(14c) Nee
  ('No')

Addition of marked prominence, whether emphatic or contrastive, will put restrictions on what can be taken as 'focus', and accordingly alters the relation between 'focus' and 'presupposition'. The question

(13a) Liep JAN op the grasveld?

will normally be answered in such a way that from the answer it appears that the presupposition is understood to have been 'somebody's walking on the grass'. The answer may be for instance

(14d) Nee, PIET
  ('No, PETER was')

but not

*(14b') Nee, hij liep op het VOETPAD
  ('No, he walked on the FOOTHPATH')

Similarly, a question like

(13b) Liep Jan op het GRASVELD?

will be answered in a way that indicates that 'John's walking on something, or, somewhere' is understood to be the presupposition, e.g., with

(14b') Nee, hij liep op het VOETPAD
  ('No, he walked on the FOOTHPATH')

but not with

*(14d) Nee, PIET
  ('No, PETER was')

I do not wish to imply that this approach solves all the complex problems of the discourse function of prominence, and I do certainly not wish to imply that questions always unambiguously determine their possible answers. Thus, the Dutch question

(15) LIEP Jan nou over het ijs?
      (lit. *'WALKED John on the ice?')

can imply both

(15a) Was John WALKING on the ice? (or was he skating?)

and

(15b) DID John walk on the ice? (or did he not?)

which cannot be distinguished in Dutch so readily as they can in English, since no separate constituents are available to indicate either the grammatical or the lexical aspects.

  In any case, the analysis of (13) and (14), above, suggests that the demarcation line between inherent prominence on the one hand and emphatic or contrastive prominence on the other hand is far less clear than has sometimes been assumed. It would suggest, in particular, that contrastive intonation under its usual definition, is in fact only a special case of emphasis or of a quite general feature of 'topicalization'.

2.2.2.3. *Syntactic and thematic function: some examples*

  Even when various factors of language use that may determine the actual intonation contour of a sentence, are left aside, it cannot be overlooked that each sentence has, not only a grammatical structure, but also what may be called a 'thematic' organization, in the sense that, semantically, one part of the sentence functions as 'what is spoken about' and one part of the sentence as 'what is said about it'. Various pairs of terms have been used as labels for this thematic organization: 'Subject' and 'Predicate' – which gives rise to a marked confusion since the same terms are also often used for syntactic analysis –, 'Topic' and 'Comment' or 'Psychological subject' and 'Psychological predicate', or 'Presupposition' and 'Focus'. Intonation serves to indicate, to the extent that this is possible, both this thematic organization and syntactic structure, which has its consequences for the description of the intonational correlates of syntax.

  For a brief illustration of the entanglements which an analysis of the grammatical rôle of intonation in isolated sentences may lead to, consider the Dutch equivalent of (1) above

(16) Hij sloeg de man met de stok

which can mean 'he gave the man a blow with the stick' or 'the man with the stick was given a blow by him'. As in the foregoing, I will be concerned with the intonational contour of sentence (16) above as a 'neutral' declarative sentence. The intonational contour corresponding to the first interpretation paraphrased above will be referred to as contour (I) and the intonational contour corresponding to the second interpretation as contour (II).

I will assume that there is at least one intonational contour which does not resolve the potential ambiguity of (16). This contour may be represented, following the conventions used earlier, as

(16) Hij sloég de màn met de stók

and will be referred to as contour (0). Let us assume, furthermore, that there is a possibility of indicating the alternative constituent structure of (16) by differences in intonation, so that it will be interpreted as either

(16a) Hij sloeg de man / met de stok
    ('He hit the man / with the stick')

or as

(16b) Hij sloeg / de man met de stok
    ('He hit / the man with the stick')

Whether or not this will typically happen in cases where there are not sufficient cues for disambiguation, or whether it is unnecessary that the occurrence of contrasting intonations be determined by the presence of a need to differentiate is a question I will leave undecided here.

The most natural way of indicating the constituent structure that goes with the interpretation (16a) would be a prominence and pitch contour that suggests — but not: causes — a slight pause after *man*:

(Ia) Hij sloèg de mân met de stók

Compare:

(17) Hij snèed het vleês met het més
    ('He cut the meat with the knife')

(18) Hij pàkte het kînd bij de hánd
    ('He took the child's hand')

What the exact levels of prominence are is not so important, as long as the prominence on the Object NP's *man, vlees, kind,* is relatively lower than the prominence on the Verbal forms *sloeg, sneed,* and *pakte,* and as long as the

Subject NP, the Verb, and the Object NP together are marked off as a sequence by the relatively higher prominence on the Adverbial phrase.

To indicate the constituent structure of the alternative interpretation (16b), however, is not so easy. A Noun Phrase like *de man met de stok* will normally have a prominence distribution with the Noun in the Complement marked and the Head Noun relatively unmarked:

(19) De màn met de stók kwam voorbìj
  ('The man with the stick came along')

or

(19) De mân met de stòk kwam voorbíj

Compare

(20) Het huìs aan de grácht wordt verkòcht
  ('The house on the canal is for sale')

or

(20) Het hûis aan de gràcht word verkócht

There is a suggestion by Stockwell (1962, quoted in Lieberman 1967:115), that in the English sentence

(21) They decorated the girl with the flowers

the Adnominal interpretation of *with the flowers* can be indicated as follows

$$\overset{2\ \ 3}{\text{(21) They décorated}} \mid \overset{2\quad 2}{\text{the girl with}} \overset{3\ \ 1}{\text{the flówers}}$$

where 3 is the highest level of prominence. I am not able to judge the English example, but for its Dutch equivalents this representation has the disadvantage that it is not altogether natural. The break in tone contour suggested by the symbol | and the distribution of prominences, in a sentence like

$$\overset{2\ \ 3}{\text{(16) Hij sloeg}} \mid \overset{2}{\text{de man met}} \overset{3}{\text{de stok}}$$

can just as well be interpreted as

(16c) Hij sloeg: de man met de stok

which, of course, is not what was intended.

The same objection is to be raised against Lieberman's alternative proposal that sentences like (21) can be disambiguated by alternative division in 'breath-groups'. By breath-group, Lieberman refers to a prosodic pattern that characteristically delimits the boundaries of unemphatic, declarative sentences. This is articulatorally correlated with 'a coordinated pattern of muscular activity that includes the subglottal, laryngeal and supraglottal muscles during an entire expiration' (p. 104). By a 'marked breath-group' is meant a similar prosodic unit, which, however, has a terminal non-falling fundamental frequency contour, by which it is marked against the normal breath-group that is typified by the falling contour at the end of a declarative sentence. It is Lieberman's assumption that in cases such as presented by (21) above, that part of the sentence which can be called the 'phonemic phrase' or 'phonological phrase' − a relatively autonomous sub-unit of prosody − can be indi-, cated by a marked breath-group, or, that such sentences can be disambiguated by a division of the speech signal 'into segments that acoustically manifest 'breaks' in the constituent structure of the derived phrase-marker' (ibid., p. 110). The assumption is not that such a breath-group division will *always* occur in an ambiguous constituent structure, or that breath-groups will always exactly correspond with grammatically definable constituents.

Even with these restrictions, I think it is implausible that the alternative organization of a sequence as in (16) will normally be indicated by a device which essentially amounts to a pause and the initiation of another respiration:

(21) They decorated / the girl with the flowers
$\quad\ \ 2\quad\ \ 3\qquad\ 2\ 2\qquad\quad\ 3\qquad 1$

Though it is possible in itself, such a way of indicating the alternative interpretations will, in normal conversational style, be interpreted as the introduction of a stylistically highly marked register of over-emphasis or over-accuracy. Nor is it plausible that more than one breath-group will be uttered in a relatively short sentence such as (16) above[14].

One way to indicate that in the interpretation (16b), *de man met de stok* is to be taken as one phonological phrase is, to change the prominence on *man* which will be accompanied by a relative lowering of prominence on *hij sloeg* as well:

(IIa) Hij sloèg de màn met de stók

Compare

(22) Hij pàkte de dòos met de fóto's
('He took the box with the pictures')

(23) Hij kèek naar het hùis aan de grácht
('He looked at the house on the canàl')

---

[14] For other criticisms of this concept, see Bierwisch (1966:107, fn. 14, and 132, fn. 37) and Kim (1968:835−6).

This contour (IIa), however, is in fact identical with at least one of the possible non-neutral or emphatic contours of the interpretation (16b):

(Ib) Hij sloèg de màn met de STOK

namely, in the sense 'what did he hit the man with? with the STICK'. The reason is the marked prominence of *met de stok* in both cases.

Similarly, another contour to indicate the interpretation (16b), where the prominence on *hij sloeg* is preserved and the prominence of *de man* and of *met de stok* are both lowered to indicate that they form one sequence:

(IIb) Hij sloég de mân met de stòk

is undistinguishable from another non-neutral contour of (16a):

(Ic) Hij SLOEG de mân met de stòk

namely, in the sense 'what did he do to the man with his stick? He HIT him with it'.

Nor is this confusion unnatural or unexplainable. We have seen that the intonation of a sentence can serve to indicate both grammatical structure and thematic organization. And the feature which plays a conspicuous rôle in terms of 'thematic' organization in (16), *and under both interpretations*, is the fact that *de man* indicates that there is some contextually defined 'man', or at least, it indicates that such a state of affairs is presupposed. For that reason, *de man* as well as other definite noun phrases can easily lose prominence, and will in many neutral intonational contours be marked inherently by a relative low prominence. Compare:

(24a) Ik hèb een bríef gezièn
('I saw a letter')

(25)   Ik héb de brièf gezién
('I saw the letter')

(24b) Ik héb een brièf gezién

The second contour, (24b) is not impossible, but carries a quite complex presupposition, like: 'You are looking for a letter? Well, I saw a letter somewhere, but...'. The same contour in (25) is quite normal: since the Noun Phrase is (+Def), the presupposition is that the letter has been 'spoken about earlier'. Compare also:

(26) Ik hèb Ján gezièn
('I saw John')

(27a) Ik héb hèm gezíen
('I saw him')

where a contour like

(27b) Ik hèb hém gezièn

is certainly emphatic.

Thus, if a sentence like (16) is uttered with a relatively low prominence on *sloeg* and *man*, to mark *met de stok* as separate, this can be interpreted, in terms of presuppositions, in two ways. Either the presupposition is: 'he hit the man', or the presupposition is: 'he hit some man'. If it is spoken with a relatively high prominence on *sloeg*, it can, in terms of presuppositions, be interpreted either as: 'he did something to the man with the stick', or as: 'he did something with his stick to the man'. Neither contour, therefore, resolves the syntactic ambiguity.

In a sentence like

(28) Hij sloeg een man met een stok
('He hit a man with a stick')

things are quite different, since the (-Def) Noun Phrase will tend to keep its inherent prominence. A contour like

(28) Hij sloèg een mân met een stók
_____ \

to mark *met een stok* as separate, that is, as Adverbial, is hardly to be expected.

Pursuing the analysis of the intonation contour of (16) a little further, it can be noted that, as is to be expected, ambiguities increase with the introduction of markedly contrastive or emphatic intonation. Particularly, since the presence of marked centers of prominence tends to lower the prominence of the other phrases or elements. If we indicate these marked prominences, as before, by representing the elements involved by capitals, we have for instance

(16c) hij sloeg de MAN met de stok
_____ \

which can be either: 'it was the MAN he hit with his stick' or 'it was the MAN with the stick he hit, not the BOY'; or we have

(16d) hij sloeg DE MAN met DE STOK
_____ \

which may be continued with: 'en de JONGEN met z'n HAND' ('and (he hit) the boy with his hand') or with: 'en de JONGEN met de REGENjas' ('and (he hit) the boy who had a trenchcoat').

This is not to deny that correlations between grammatical structure and intonation may present themselves unambiguously in other cases. The investigation carried out by Cohen and 't Hart mentioned earlier, bears out, for instance, that there is a quite consistent difference in intonation in the Dutch sequence

(29)   Daar is een man die wil praten

that can either mean

(29a) Daar is een man die wil praten
        ('There is a man who wants to talk')

or

(29b) Daar is een man. Die wil praten.
        ('There is a man. He wants to talk').

This involves a relatively small shift in the point where the fall of the pitch contour begins at the end of the sequence *Daar is een man*. If the fall starts later, this gives the suggestion of a continuation, as in (29a); if the fall starts earlier, this suggests the decline of pitch contour typical for the end of a declarative sentence, as in (29b). The same intonational feature also plays a rôle in the difference between so-called restrictive and non-restrictive relative clauses. The sentences

(30a) De man die getuige was van het ongeluk, wordt gezocht
        ('The man who witnessed the accident is looked for')
(30b) De man, die getuige was van het ongeluk, wordt gezocht
        ('The man, who witnessed the accident, is looked for')

will often be distinguished by marked differences in intonation. This, incidentally, reinforces the viewpoint that the 'non-restrictive' relative clause in these cases has in fact the function of an apposition or a second sentence. Similarly, there are cases of potential ambiguity of coordination that may be disambiguated by intonation, especially when a difference like the one between 'continued' vs. 'non-continued' contours are involved.

But this does not alter the fact that the case for this ambiguation by grammatical intonation is weak, or at least much weaker than the case against it. From the admittedly few examples investigated above, the reasons appear to be the following.

(i) The function of sentence intonation is as much to indicate syntactic structure as to indicate discourse function.

(ii) This leads to ambiguities that will most of the time go unnoticed in discourse, since from discourse one will generally be able to infer the presuppositions and other factors that have an influence on intonation.

(iii) For that very reason, however, an unambiguous correlation between syntactic structure and intonational contours in each individual sentence will often be absent. One might even conclude that the investigation of sentence intonation from the strictly grammatical point of view is artificial and unpromising.

2.3. Some conclusions

The problem of junctures and intonation has been posed here first of all because there always has been much discussion over the question as to whether grammatically ambiguous sentences are, strictly speaking, ambiguous, or whether prosodic features serve to distinguish the alternative structures. I have tried to demonstrate (i) that the rôle of prosody in this respect is of necessity limited and therefore, the claim that sentences of the kind discussed above are not 'really' ambiguous in linguistic description is unwarranted (ii) that the viewpoint that, in actual speech, the linguistic context or the situation in general will 'trigger' the intended prosodic realization or interpretation is simplistic inasmuch as context may very well have the opposite result.

It would appear, then, that the problem of the interrelation between prosodic structure and grammatical structure is still very much unresolved. Paradoxically enough, one reason for this is that these matters have first and foremost been approached from a strictly 'phonological' viewpoint and that the question has been put in terms of 'minimal pairs', which had hindered the investigation of the nature and function of prosody to a considerable extent. It is also the reason why many of the standard examples from the literature on juncture are so highly implausible in terms of meaningful contrast. They can serve to illustrate standpoints on the relation between sound and grammar, but they are hardly suitable for an investigation of actual disambiguation.

Pending the outcome of differently oriented investigations, I think we are justified in assuming that the rôle of prosody does not really affect the problem of ambiguity in natural language inasmuch as in the majority of cases of language use the 'unmarked' realization of ambiguous sentences will be the normal one. I will therefore, in the following chapters, ignore the fact that prosodic features may be involved in some of the examples presented.

3. AMBIGUITY AND GRAMMAR: THE CONCEPT OF HOMO-NYMY

3.1. Preliminary remarks

The term 'grammar' will be used here for what is traditionally called morphology and syntax, and not for the linguistic description in its entirety, as the term is used in Transformational grammar and Stratificational grammar.

As said before in chapter 1 (p. 10), a sentence like

(1) They are flying planes

will be regarded as grammatically homonymous. To this sentence, more than one grammatical structure can be assigned, corresponding to the alternative interpretations 'certain people are engaged in flying certain objects' and 'certain objects are planes that fly' respectively. Under the one interpretation, (1) above can be divided into a Nominal Constituent *they*, a Verb Phrase *are flying* and a Nominal Constituent *planes*. Under the second interpretation, *flying planes* in a Nominal Constituent in the Predicate Phrase *are flying planes*.

This difference in constituent structure can be correlated with a difference in grammatical function: under the first interpretation, *planes* is Object to the Predicator *are flying*, under the second interpretation, *flying planes* is a Predicate Complement to the Predicator *are*; under both interpretations, *they* is Subject. The use of these functional labels is traditional, and no claims are implied by their employment here, which is solely on the ground of their usefulness. On a finer level of grammatical categorization, the two occurrences of *they* in the two interpretations of sentence (1), can be distinguished as Agentive vs. Non-Agentive, whereas *planes* can be called Non-Ergative in both grammatical structures[1].

On the level of lexical description, *are flying* in the first interpretation and *flying* in the second will be regarded as different forms of the same lexical element, or lexeme, FLY; whether *are* in the Predicate Phrase *are/flying planes* is a form of a lexeme BE or just a 'verbalizer' is open to debate. In general, sentences that, grammatically, are homonymous may contain constituents that are lexically the 'same'; in point of fact, this is one of the major motivations for introducing the notion of grammatical homonymy. To quote another well-known example of Chomsky's, the sentence

[1] For some recent suggestions in this direction, see Fillmore (1968), Lyons (1968: 350 ff.), and Anderson (1968a).

57

(2) The shooting of the hunters was terrible

has two interpretations which can be paraphrased as 'the shooting by the hunters was terrible' and 'the hunters getting shot was terrible'. This can be most readily explained by the assumption that the phrase *the shooting of the hunters* represents two different grammatical relations, 'Subjective' in the first case and 'Objective' in the second case. The lexical elements SHOOT and HUNTER are identical in each case. Nor does it seem promising to attribute the difference in grammatical structure or in interpretation to a different meaning of the element *of*. Such relatively uninformative elements as *of* should rather be viewed upon as syntactic elements that, precisely because their contribution to the total meaning of the sentence is rather small, can function as members of constructions expressing different relations; they should not be viewed as 'homonymous' or 'polysemous' elements themselves.

On the other hand, the ambiguity of the sentence

(3) The bank was the scene of the crime

will here be regarded as a case of lexical ambiguity. (3) contains homonymous lexical elements *bank* ('place for depositing money' or 'bank of a river'), and in this sentence, *bank* could mean either the one or the other. The grammatical structure of (3), however, is the same under both interpretations.

A distinction will thus be maintained between, on the one hand, the description of lexical elements like PLANE, FLY, HUNTER, SHOOT, and on the other hand the description of grammatical constructions, grammatical functions like Subject, Object, Agent, and other grammatical categories such as Tense, Number, Mood. I will without further discussion assume that such a distinction is useful, though of course many problems are involved in it. One of these problems, the interrelatedness between grammatical and lexical structure will be dealt with as the discussion develops.

3.1.1. *The sentence*
A grammatical description is, in the first place, concerned with sentences. I will pass over the problem of a definition of the sentence here. As sentences will be regarded utterance types to which at least one grammatical structure can be assigned, in accordance with traditional practice.

This traditional notion poses two problems. One is that there are expressions like *Who? Me?*, *Two, please, Rather not,* that should not be excluded from linguistic description. The other is, that there are sequences of sentences like *Mary was afraid that John would hear about it. Therefore she did not tell him,* from which it appears that there can also be grammatical relations *between* sentences. Though the sentence as it is usually understood, seems to be the best starting point for a linguistic description, it has rightly been observed, e.g., by Pike (1967[2]:145–8; 464–6) that it is arbitrary to restrict linguistic or even grammatical description to the traditional 'sentences'. For a proper account of such universal phenomena as anaphoric reference and coordination, that restriction will eventually prove to be untenable (see Dik 1968a:164 ff.). We have seen above (chapter 2), that an investigation of the intonation of sentences automatically involves their discourse function.

As for the problem of such expressions as *Two, please* and the fact that, as units, they are comparable to the traditional sentence, it can be expected that a proper definition of a notion 'linguistic expression' which covers both such expressions and sentences will have to rely upon other criteria than grammatical structure, and most prominently on criteria from intonation[2].

As appears from the formulation 'at least one grammatical structure', above, I will use the term sentence both for utterance types that have one grammatical structure and for utterance types that have more than one. I thus take exception to the terminology introduced in Katz and Postal (1964:24–5), and thereafter used in some other Transformational publications where examples such as (1) and (2) above are referred to as 'sentences' — terminal strings of formatives which represent more than one 'sentoid' — a terminal string of formatives with its unique structural description. This terminology is unfortunate (see Dik 1968a:241; also Weinreich 1966b:418, fn. 41). The suffix *-oid*, for once, usually indicates a phenomenon that, though similar to another phenomenon, is only defectively or partially identical with it. Since the term 'sentence' is traditionally related to the notion 'utterance type with its grammatical structure', it is unnatural to speak of a 'sentoid' in all cases when a string of elements has only one grammatical structure, and to use the term 'sentence' to refer to a string of elements that, strictly speaking, only has a shape, and not a grammatical structure.

In fact, I would prefer to speak of two (or more) 'sentences' in cases of grammatical homonymy; but since the criteria for homonymy are the issue here, I will use the term 'sentence' as defined above. This might seem to imply that sentences that represent more than one grammatical structure are regarded as a special category, and that is exactly what will be maintained here.

---

[2] This point has always been stressed by Reichling, see e.g. Reichling (1969[5]:26–7). Bierwisch (1966:110) proposes to formulate the sentence-boundaries in such a fashion that not only 'reduced' or 'elliptical' sentences but also answers like *No*, or *Last week*, will automatically receive the intonation features of 'sentences'.

Contrary to for instance Kraak (1966:52–3) who maintains that homonymous sentences are not a special category for native speakers, I will assume that they are, both for the linguistic description and for native speakers.

As for the first point, this in my opinion follows by definition. Under the assumption that a linguistic description assigns a grammatical structure to sentences, it follows that such cases where more than one grammatical structure is assigned to the same sentence, are of a different nature. This does not rule out the possibility that linguistic descriptions will differ in the extent to which they regard sentences as 'homonymous'; in fact, this is one of the major problems connected with the use of the term. Another and complementary problem is that a sentence can have the same grammatical structure and still be ambiguous. But it would seem to me that in any format of linguistic description homonymy is the exception; if it is not, the term 'homonymous' becomes useless and should be replaced by the vaguer term 'ambiguous'.

The widely recognized fact that in actual speech homonymy will in most cases be automatically resolved and often even go unnoticed, is an entirely different matter. We are concerned here with homonymous sentence-types, as a category in the linguistic description, and not with homonymous sentences as utterance-tokens. Moreover, such familiar phenomena as deliberate or accidental punning, and other communicative effects of homonymous or otherwise ambiguous sentences, support the assumption that for native speakers too, such sentences do have special characteristics, which can be elicited under proper circumstances.

Psycholinguistic research on this matter (see MacKay 1966; MacKay and Bever 1967) points to the conclusion that the presence of ambiguities in sentences interferes with native speakers' interpretational abilities, even when they are not positively aware of the ambiguities. It may also provoke significant reactions like giggling and stuttering.

In a test described in MacKay (1966), speakers were asked to complete two types of sentences, one of which was potentially ambiguous, like

Although he mentioned the problems with the bishop, ...

These fragments were mixed with almost identical, but unambiguous fragments of sentences, like

Although he mentioned the problems to the bishop, ...

It appeared that the 'completion time' for the potentially ambiguous fragments was significantly longer, and that the ambiguities interfered in other ways also, for instance with the nature of the completion. In some cases, the completion of the potentially ambiguous fragments was markedly illogical. A test described in MacKay and Bever (1967) points to the conclusion that the 'perception time' for ambiguous sentences is to a certain extent a function of the type of ambiguity they present (lexical or grammatical ambiguity, single ambiguity or double ambiguity). In particular, it should be noted that MacKay's experimental data lead him to the tentative hypothesis that native speakers are less able to assign an interpretation to an ambiguous sentence properly as long as they have not realized that the sentence *is* ambiguous[2a].

One should, of course, be careful with admitting evidence from psycholinguistic research in the defence of one view of linguistic description against another; for instance, in larger contexts things may be quite different from what they were in the test-situation. Even so, in view of the phenomena mentioned above, and of the attention ambiguity has attracted from antiquity onwards, and also in view of the rôle the concept of homonymy usually plays in discussions of linguistic description, Kraak's claim that there is no reason to assume that homonymous sentences are a special category is a rather curious one[3].

I certainly do *not* wish to maintain, however, that all sentences that could receive more than one interpretation are therefore 'homonymous' in the sense that more than one grammatical structure has to be assigned to them, or in the sense that they are a-typical. As said before, it will on the contrary be one of the basic viewpoints defended here that a distinction must be made between sentences that are inherently ambiguous in the sense that they are grammatically homonymous, sentences that are assigned to the 'same' grammatical structure but still could be assigned more than one 'meaning' in the description, and sentences that are not inherently ambiguous but might nevertheless, in actual discourse, be interpreted in more than one way. This, eventually, entails that a distinction should be made also between the inherent meaning of a sentence and its final interpretation by native speakers.

[2a] Some of MacKay's claims have since been challenged, but there is as yet no reason to abandon the hypothesis that ambiguities interfere with the perception of sentences (see Garrett 1970).

[3] Kraak here opposes the 'contextual' view of homonymy and observes that it is inconceivable that context should introduce structures that are not already present. On this, I agree with him (though it is another question as to whether it is true in all cases of ambiguity). This entails that, in terms of competence, a native speaker is capable of assigning more than one grammatical structure to a sentence, and in terms of performance, that he is capable of selecting one of these structures as context or situation require. I fail to see how the conclusion can be avoided that, in terms of competence, there is a 'choice' involved in those cases — which Kraak denies. The fact that in most cases no speaker is aware of this — though in puns we certainly are — and that we are as yet ignorant about the nature of such a 'selection' does not alter the fact.

3.2. Homonymy and grammatical description

Of late, sentences like (1) and (2) above have been widely used for diagnostic and heuristic purposes in grammatical description, and for the illustration of basic assumptions in grammatical theory and of linguistic theory in general. This is especially true of Transformational-generative grammar, where the phenomenon of 'grammatical homonymy' has from the start been adduced to point out shortcomings of phrase structure grammars[4], and subsequently to underline the importance of the distinction between 'deep structure' and 'surface structure'[5].

In the theory of semantic description proposed in Katz and Fodor (1964), equal weight is put on the detection and the resolution of ambiguities that such a theory should be capable of [6]. And although his theory is in some respects different in outlook and he also employs another model of description in some crucial points, various writings of McCawley (see for instance McCawley 1970) are also abundantly illustrated with ambiguities that to an extent determine what structure a particular sentence should receive in the description.

It is no exaggeration to state, that in general the degree to which a grammatical description is capable of recognizing that otherwise identical sequences of linguistic elements are homonymous and should be assigned to more than one grammatical structure, has become one of the major tests for the adequacy of such a description, and also, that this is largely due to the impact of Transformational grammar.

Chomsky, however, already in *Syntactic Structures* (1957:86, fn. 1)[7]

---

[4] See, for one example out of hundreds, Chomsky (1957:88 ff.), on the ambiguity of *the shooting of the hunters*.

[5] Chomsky (1965:15 ff.). Compare also various remarks in Chomsky (1966, especially p. 54 ff.), where it is argued that the comments by Vaugelas on the French 'subjective' and 'objective' genitive can be understood in terms of 'deep' vs. 'surface' grammar. But see Zimmer (1968, especially p. 299 ff.).

[6] See for instance p. 485: '(...) one facet of the speaker's ability that a semantic theory will have to reconstruct is that he can detect non-syntactic ambiguities and characterize the content of each reading of a sentence'. Cf. also p. 493: 'The semantic interpretations assigned by the projection rules operating on grammatical and dictionary information (...) must mark each semantic ambiguity a speaker can detect'.

[7] 'In his 'Two models of grammatical description' Hockett uses notions of structural ambiguity to demonstrate the independence of various linguistic notions in a manner very similar to what we are suggesting here'. Cf. also Chomsky (1967a:441, fn. 32): 'Modern linguistics has made occasional use of this property of language as a research tool. The first general discussion of how ambiguity can be used to illustrate the inadequacy of certain conceptions of syntactic structure is in C.F.Hockett's 'Two models for [read: of] grammatical description'.'

credits Immediate Constituent analysis with having first brought to attention the importance of 'constructional homonymy' for grammatical theory. The standard case is the analysis of the phrase

(4) old men and women (were left at the village)

in Wells (1947) and in Hockett (1954).

As to other schools of linguistic description, 'homonymy' plays a rôle too in Tagmemics, but a far less important one. In Pike's view[8] a homonymous sentence or phrase is an utterance that accidentally represents two contrasting tagmeme sequences, and ambiguity is a feature of language use rather than an essential property of sentences. In his view of linguistic description, the ambiguity of a linguistic element on a particular level x will be partially resolved on a one higher level $x+1$, and the unresolved ambiguities on the level $x+1$ will be partially resolved on the one higher level $x+2$, and so forth; on the level of the sentence, residual ambiguities will more often than not be resolved on the level of discourse. A description of such a gradual resolution of ambiguities can be found in Callow (1968)[9].

In Stratificational grammar, the homonymy problem appears under the terms 'neutralization' vs. 'diversification', and is not restricted to the sentence level. Two or more contrasting elements on one level, say, the past participle 'lexon' and the past tense 'lexon' in English, on a lower level may be represented by the same element -ed. The recognition of such a neutralization leads to an operation referred to as 'vertical splitting' (see e.g. Lamb 1966:5). Though neutralization is a crucial concept in Lamb's format of description in terms of levels or rather, strata, the terms 'homonymous' and 'ambiguous' in Stratificational grammar are, at least in practice, not nearly as widely applied as they are in Transformational grammar[10].

Still, it appears that in spite of fundamental mutual differences of emphasis, it is felt to be necessary and expedient in various schools of grammatical description to regard some sentences as 'homonymous', 'homophonous' or 'homomorphic'. This being so, two questions can be raised:

---

[8] Compare Pike (1967[2]:231 fn. 8): '... ambiguous utterances are treated as homophonous sentences (or phrases) via homophonous manifesting morphemes of contrasting tagmeme sequences'.

[9] Examples of the 'matrix technique' for resolving neutralizations in grammatical constructions are to be found in Pike and Erickson (1964) and Pike (1963). See also chapter 1, p. 7).

[10] In a different context, grammatical homonymy is discussed in Stutterheim (1965[2]; see especially chapter 10, 'Structuur of betekenis?', p. 119 ff.).

(i) Why are some sentences of a language viewed as grammatically having more than one structure?
(ii) Under what conditions is it proper to assign more than one grammatical structure to one and the 'same' sentence, and under what conditions is it not?

As for the first question, its answer may, very generally, be formulated as follows: a grammatical description that is not capable of assigning more than one grammatical structure to some sentences is inadequate. The second question has to my knowledge been discussed less extensively. Both questions, however, have been treated in a fundamental manner in Hockett (1954), and I will therefore go into his arguments in more detail.

3.2.1. *Hockett's view*
Consider again the sentence

(4) Old men and women were left at the village.

There are two possible interpretations, that can be paraphrased as

(4a) Women were left at the village and old men were left at the village

and

(4b) Old men were left at the village and old women were left at the village

respectively. The solution proposed by Wells (1947:194—5) within the 'Item-and-Arrangement' framework of Immediate Constituent analysis is the following. Under the interpretation (4a), the phrase *old men and women* has the construction

$$N(Phr)+and+N(Phr),$$

where the first N(Phr) in turn belongs to the construction Mod+N(Phr). Under the interpretation (4b) the phrase *old men and women* has the construction

$$Mod+N(Phr)$$

where the N(Phr) in turn belongs to the construction

$$N(Phr)+and+N(Phr).$$

Or, in terms of 'constructional meaning', the phrase *old men and women* in (4a) has the meaning of the conjunction-construction N(Phr) *and* N(Phr); in (4b) it has the meaning of the Modifier-Head construction Mod + N(Phr).

It has been pointed out since that this solution is unsatisfactory because under the interpretation (4b), *old* does not modify the conjunction (*men and women*), as it does in Wells' description, but rather modifies both the coordinated Nouns *men* and *women*. Furthermore, there are coordinated Noun Phrases for which it *is* true that the Predicate Complement modifies the conjunction rather than its members. This can be illustrated with sentences like

(5) John and Mary are a nice pair

vs.

(6) John and Mary are erudite.

A similar difference can be attested in sentences with plural Noun Phrases. We have

(7) The rival firms finally came to an agreement

vs.

(8) The old firms finally gave up the struggle.

In (7), the natural interpretation is: the rival firms made an agreement with each other, in (8) the natural interpretation is: the old firms each individually gave up the struggle.

In this respect, Wells' analysis of the phrase *old men and women* in (4) can be regarded as one illustration of the fact that IC analysis is unable to account for various differences of 'scope' (see Dik 1968a: 227 ff.). For an analysis of sentences containing plural Noun Phrases, see McCawley (1968a) and Hudson (1970)[11]. On the other hand, the transformational solution originally proposed for sentences such as (4), in which the interpretation (4b) was accounted for by a derivation of the phrase *old men and women* from underlying structures corresponding to 'the men be old' and 'the women be old',' has for cases like (5) and (7) met with serious difficulties that have been discussed at length in Dik (1968a), Dougherty (1968), and McCawley (1968a).

It is, however, not this particular problem of grammatical description that will concern us here, but the conclusion drawn by Hockett (1954: 391) in his discussion of Wells' example. Hockett's argument, to which I will essentially subscribe in this section, runs as follows: Sentence (4) has two clearly different interpretations. To these correspond two different 'hierarchical structures'. This difference in 'hierarchical structure' is not to be derived from a difference between the individual morphemes and words, since these are the

---

[11] However, Hudson's article also illustrates the problem of to what extent an ambiguity in one type of grammatical construction is equivalent to an ambiguity in another type of construction.

same under both interpretations. Nor is it to be derived from linear arrangement, since this is the same under both interpretations too. The difference in hierarchical structure, however, can be accounted for if we say that under the one interpretation sentence (4) represents a grammatical structure A, and under the other interpretation sentence (4) represents a grammatical structure B. This, furthermore, is a legitimate step to take, since there is a class of sentences with different words and morphemes that represent the same structure A, and there is another class of sentences with other words and morphemes that represent the same structure B. To these sentences is assigned the grammatical structure A, say, Modifier-Head, in the one case, and the grammatical structure B, say, Conjunction, in the other case, even though they may contain different words and morphemes. Hence, a linguistic description can follow this procedure for a sentence like (4), and assign to it two different 'hierarchical structures', although they contain the same words and morphemes.

It is not the meaning of (4), in the sense of the speaker's intention or the hearer's interpretation, that determines its grammatical structure: sentences such as (4) have two different 'hierarchical structures' and therefore can be understood in more than one way. In particular, sentences such as (4) do not have at the same time *both* structure A *and* structure B; from the viewpoint of a grammatical description they have *either* structure A *or* structure B. But since these two disjoint grammatical structures are represented by a sentence that is 'same' as far as the words and morphemes it contains is concerned and its linear arrangement, it also follows that there may be instances of language use where such sentences are meant or understood to be 'ambiguous' in the sense that they do mean two things 'at the same time'.

Cases such as (4) are therefore particularly appropriate for demonstrating a fact of much wider implications, namely that 'hierarchical structure' is a primitive of the linguistic description just as much as 'linear arrangement' is. To demonstrate this, in fact, is one of the main purposes of Hockett's article. Though he presents his analysis and his arguments in the framework of phrase structure grammar, I will assume that in principle his line of reasoning is valid for other formats of grammatical description as well, and will henceforth replace his notion 'hierarchical structure' with the more general 'grammatical structure'[12].

The answer to the first question posed above (p. 64), of why some sentences should have more than one grammatical structure assigned to them, can now be formulated as follows: whenever a grammatical description is con-

[12] Compare also Hockett's notion 'deep grammar' in Hockett (1958: 246 ff.).

fronted with a sentence that has more than one interpretation, and whenever these interpretations can be accounted for by mapping that sentence onto two (or more than two) different grammatical structures, a linguistic description should make this 'either-or' solution, rather than assuming that the sentence under consideration has one and only one grammatical structure (the 'neither-nor' solution). It should be emphasized that in this latter solution, which does not recognize homonymy, one is of course still under the obligation to explain the difference in interpretation.

As for the second question posed, the conditions under which one can take recourse to the concept of 'homonymy' in a grammatical description follow from the answer to the first question: if in a grammatical description, more than one structure, let us say, structures A and B, are assigned to one and the same sentence, there should be other sentences in that same language which within the framework of that same grammatical description unambiguously have the grammatical structure A, and other sentences, which unambiguously have the grammatical structure B. This is trivial inasfar as that when a grammatical description makes a choice, there should be something to choose from. It is not trivial at all, however, if it is taken as a condition which prevents ad-hoc grammatical categories from being introduced to account for an ambiguity; I will try to demonstrate that it should be interpreted as such a condition.

3.2.2. *Homonymy, constituent structure, and grammatical relations*

Thus, the first reason why a grammatical description makes use of the concept of homonymy is not that different interpretations of the same sentence can be explained in this way. This first reason is rather that a grammatical description that did not want to view some sentences as homonymous would face considerable difficulties. The arguments for this have become quite familiar now, and I will illustrate this point only briefly.

Consider again a sentence that contains a prepositional phrase, such as

(1) He hit the man with the stick.

This sentence clearly has two different interpretations. Under the one interpretation, *with the stick* is an Adjunct in the Noun Phrase *the man with the stick*, under the other interpretation it is a Complement to the Predicate Phrase *hit the man*. Or, in traditional terminology, under the one interpretation on *with the stick* has an Adjectival function, under the second interpretation it has an Adverbial function. In this respect, sentence (1) does not stand alone, since we have such cases as

(2) He cut the meat on the table
(3) They decorated the girl with the flowers
(4) He never fought a bull with real courage

where the prepositional phrases all share the feature that they can belong
either to the second Noun Phrase or to the Predicate Phrase as Adverbial Complements. Besides these sentences there are others which, for various reasons,
are not ambiguous in this respect. For example, the sentences

(5) He cut the meat on a table
(6) They decorated her with the flowers
(7) He fought two bulls with his bare hands

all contain prepositional phrases that will be taken as Adverbial. In the examples

(8) The meat on the table is not fresh
(9) The girl with the flowers is my niece
(10) A bull with real courage sometimes is less dangerous

the prepositional phrases will, on the contrary, be taken as Adjectival. As in
many cases of constructional homonymy, the presence of two alternative
grammatical structures within one and the same sentence can here be illustrated by a change in word-order. Compare also

(11) On the table he cut the meat
(12) With the flowers they decorated the girl
(13) With real courage he fought a bull

where the prepositional phrases are Adverbial only.

If a grammatical description states that under the one interpretation sentence (1) represents a structure A, and under the other interpretation it represents a structure B, it thereby has the possibility of making several statements
at once. Firstly, it gives a reasonable account of the interpretational difference
by saying that in the first case the prepositional phrase is a Nominal Adjunct
and in the second case a Verbal Complement. Secondly, the same statement
applies to the examples (2), (3), and (4), so that a similar multiple meaning is
accounted for in the same way. Thirdly, the description shows that the grammatical structure A, present in (1) to (4) is also the grammatical structure of
(8), (9) and (10), and that the grammatical structure B, present in (1) to (4)
is also the grammatical structure of (5), (6) and (7). This enables the grammatical description to state that sentences can have the same grammatical structure in spite of the fact that neither the order of words and word groups nor

the lexical elements themselves are identical. Fourthly, once the difference in constituent structure is shown for examples (1) to (4), the difference in grammatical function of the Nominal Adjunct and the Verbal Complement can be explained by the statement that in the grammatical structure A the *with*-phrase is a post-nominal Modifier, and that in the grammatical structure B the *with*-phrase has the function 'Instrumental'. In (2), the prepositional phrase, though equally Adverbial, has the function 'Place', and in (4) the prepositional phrase, though it is similar to the one in (3) in that it is Adverbial and contains the preposition *with*, has the function 'Manner'. This, finally, enables the grammatical description to illustrate on a few examples that grammatical structure is not in one-to-one correspondence with linear arrangement and that grammatical function is not in one-to-one correspondence with constituent structure.

Imagine on the other hand, a grammar that would not want to describe (1) as grammatically homonymous. Such a grammar would assign one and the same constituent structure to this sentence for instance by taking *with the stick* as just a prepositional Complement. By this it would already have missed the opportunity to generalize the similarities between (1) and (2), (3) and (4), and to make a general statement about the similarities and the differences between these four sentences and the sentences (8), (9) and (10) on the one hand and the sentences (5), (6) and (7) on the other hand. Also, *with the stick* will, under the assumption that (1) is not grammatically homonymous, be assigned to the same grammatical function, say, Complement of Circumstance. The label in itself is less important than the fact that both interpretations of (1) will then have to be explained as contextual variants of one and the same grammatical function.

By the same token, if the *with*-phrase in (1) has the same grammatical function under both interpretations, there is at least in principle no basis for assuming that the *with*-phrases have different grammatical functions in (1) and (4) or (3) and (4); these functions, too, will then have to be regarded as contextual variants of one and the same function.

The first problem with such an approach is, that statements about constituent structure cannot be made, though they are quite crucial if a grammatical description aims not only at the description of the structure of one particular sentence but also at generalizations about sentence structure. This speaks for itself.

The second problem mentioned deserves some further comment. In itself, it is not at all implausible that all the *with*-phrases in the above examples, share a feature that may be labelled 'Circumstance'. For the Adverbial phrases, whether of Place, of Manner, Time or Instrument, this was proposed in Weinreich 1966b:437. To this could be added that it is also the case that the *with*-

phrases that function as post-nominal Modifiers are in this one respect similar to the Adverbial ones. However, the label 'Circumstance', to indicate the grammatical function which these phrases have in the sentences quoted, is hardly adequate since it is too vague.

This can be argued from the comparison of sentences like (1), (3) and (4) with sentences where it *can* be assumed that the *with*-phrases have some such function as Circumstance. Compare for instance

(14) With the Americans gone, Hanoi would then be able to deal directly with Saigon
(15) Now, with the onset of moratorium week, the achievement seems to have been ephemeral
(16) For this sociology, the owl of Minerva spreads its wings only with the falling of the dusk
(17) He can't see the fish with the jar in the way[13].

I would maintain that in such sentences the *with*-phrases indeed do indicate no more than what by Schwartz has been called 'attendant circumstance', and that the different interpretations assigned to them are explainable by the sentence context.

It is perhaps tempting to say that in (14) and (17) the function of the *with*-phrase is 'Cause', and that in (15) it is 'Simultaneity'. The reason to object to such a specification is that it is unnecessary, and that unnecessary specifications should be avoided for reasons of economy of description. The fact that the position of the jar in (17) is the reason that 'he' cannot see the fish does not have to be explained by calling the *with*-phrase 'Causal' since without that it is equally clear that 'he' can't see the fish for some reason and that there is a 'Circumstance' which prevents it.

If a prepositional phrase allows such different interpretations where distinctions like 'Cause' or 'Simultaneity' will depend on data from a larger context, and if furthermore the phrase seems to be perfectly neutral in some cases as regards these distinctions, as it is in (15) for instance, it is accordingly more expedient to describe it as neutral than to describe it as inherently ambiguous or homonymous.

A similar phenomenon is present in Dutch sentences with phrases with the comparable preposition *met*: we have

(19) Ze voetbalden met slecht weer
    (lit. *'They played football with bad weather')

---

[13] The example is from Schwartz (1968:767).

which means 'At the time they played football the weather was bad'. Besides this sentence, there is the sentence

(20) Met slecht weer kunnen wij niet spelen
(Lit. *'With bad weather we cannot play').

Here the phrase *met slecht weer* again means no more than 'When the weather is bad', but in this context it will be interpreted as 'Because the weather is bad', just as in other contexts the same *met*-phrase will be interpreted as 'Though the weather is bad', etc. It is also clear, however, that in such sentences as

(1) He hit the man with the stick
(21) He frightened her with that story
(3) They decorated the girl with the flowers

the label 'Circumstance' is too vague, since despite mutual differences these phrases quite unambiguously share the feature that the activity or the result of an activity described is brought about 'by means of' that which is mentioned in the *with*-phrase. Similarly, in the examples

(23) He shut the door with a blow
(24) He fought the bull with courage
(25) He read the book with care

the three *with*-phrases share the feature that they specify the 'way' in which the activity was performed, and therefore can be labelled 'Manner'. This is not to deny that these categories can be regarded as developments of one and the same fundamental category 'Circumstance', but to illustrate that such a 'development' can reach a point where it becomes necessary to recognize that there are in fact several different categories.

The same applies to the constituent structure of the examples (1) to (13). It is plausible that in the last resort the Adverbial and the Adnominal *with*-phrases are related, but it is also quite easily demonstrable that a grammatical description which leaves it at that is unable to cope with the differences in constituent structure.

From these observations, then, I will draw the provisional conclusion that a grammatical description which views the sentence (1) in its two interpretations as 'same' both in terms of constituent structure and in terms of grammatical function is less adequate than a grammatical description that regards (1) as grammatically homonymous. The latter solution thereby, in general, recognizes two things: one, that the restrictions on the possibilities of word-order and word-group order can create ambiguities of 'scope'; two, that one and the same prepositional phrase like *with the stick* can have different grammatical functions.

It would appear that the occurrence of constructional homonymy is no more surprising in itself than the existence of lexically homonymous word-forms such as *bank*. The fact that two prepositional phrases with the same preposition are assigned different grammatical functions like Manner and Instrumental will of course, in some cases, mean that it can be disputed whether the one rather than the other grammatical relation is present. This is the case in examples like

(26) She lost paradise with her first bite of the apple
     (Schwartz 1968:770)

where it can be disputed whether the *with*-phrase indicates 'Simultaneity' or 'Cause'.

Such borderline cases are to be expected when the 'same' prepositional phrase, or, in general, the 'same' constituent, is said to fulfill different functions in different sentences. But this is a small price to pay compared to the generalizations that become possible once such a distinction is made.

3.3. Homonymy and ambiguity: Instrumental Adverbs

The remarks made above, however, are not nearly sufficient to answer all the objections that might be raised against homonymy as a descriptive device. It is hard to conceive how an approach to grammatical analysis that does not recognize homonymy could be successful in general. I believe, however, that the usefulness of such an approach does not depend so much on its absolute 'content', but on the degree to which it is applied in linguistic description. And the same in my opinion is true of the opposite view, under which different interpretations of one and the same sentence are mapped onto different grammatical structures. This is as good a moment as any to recall what I will refer to as Hockett's condition II: if, in a linguistic description, one applies the criterion of homonymy, there should be a solid reason for this, and the reason should be in the structure of the language and its sentences, rather than in the meaning of one or two isolated sentences.

The distinction, for instance, between *with the stick* as an Adnominal Complement and the same sequence as an Adverbial Complement in sentences like (1) above can be shown to be relevant in a quite straightforward manner. But such distinctions do not of necessity resolve all ambiguities.

As pointed out by Lakoff (1968), a sentence like

(28) I cut my finger with a knife

can have two different interpretations, even though *with a knife* is an Instrumental Adverbial Phrase. There is one interpretation that Lakoff calls 'accidental' and that can be paraphrased as 'I cut my finger on a knife'. There is another – perhaps in this case less probable interpretation – which Lakoff calls 'purposive' and can be paraphrased as 'I used a knife in making a cut in my finger'. Let us refer to these two interpretations as

(28a) I cut my finger with a knife (accidental)
(28b) I cut my finger with a knife (purposive).

The purposive sense is also present in a sentence like

(29) I sliced the salami with a knife.

According to Lakoff, this sentence is in fact synonymous with the sentence

(30) I used a knife to slice the salami.

He then proceeds to prove two things: (i) There are various grammatical contexts where the accidental interpretation of sentences with Adverbial *with*-phrases is ruled out, but where the purposive interpretation holds. This suggests that (28a) and (28b) are grammatically different. (ii) The selectional restrictions and co-occurrence relations of sentences of the type (29) and (30), on the other hand, are very much identical.
(i) Some contexts where according to Lakoff the accidental interpretation is impossible but the purposive interpretation is possible, are:

(31) I was cutting my finger with a knife
(32) I cut my finger without a knife
(33) Cut your finger with a knife
(34) I carefully cut my finger with a knife
(35) He forced me to cut my finger with a knife.

(ii) Identical selectional restrictions and co-occurrence relations for sentences of the type (29) and sentences of the type (30) are to be found in the following pairs:

(36) He computed the answer with a slide rule
(37) He used a slide rule to compute the answer

(38) *He knew the answer with a slide rule
(39) *He used a slide rule to know the answer

(40) John killed Harry with dynamite
(41) John used dynamite to kill Harry

(42) *The explosion killed Harry with dynamite
(43) *The explosion used dynamite to kill Harry

(44) Did Seymour slice the salami with a knife?

(45) Did Seymour use a knife to slice the salami?

(46) Seymour didn't slice the salami with a knife

(47) Seymour didn't use a knife to slice the salami

(48) *With the knife, Seymour didn't slice the salami

(49) *Seymour used the knife not to slice the salami.

Conditions of selection and co-occurrence are crucial in the definition of the level of deep structure in Transformational grammar. One of the primary criteria upon which one can decide whether or not two sentences have the same grammatical structure on this level, is to point out categorial identities of selection and co-occurrence, and one of the primary criteria upon which to decide whether or not one and the same sentence represents more than one grammatical structure is to point out basic differences in these same respects[14]

From the observations that are partially reproduced above, Lakoff concludes that a sentence like (29) is, in fact, only a surface variant of the structure underlying a sentence like (30); and, if one assumes that these two sentences have the same deep structure grammatically, the selectional restrictions and co-occurrence relations (29) and (30) share require to be stated only once in the description. Further, he argues that Instrumental Adverbs like *with a knife* in (28) do not represent a deep structure grammatical category at all. There are grammatical constraints such as the one that appears from the examples (48) and (49), that are better explained by assuming that (29) has an underlying grammatical structure corresponding to that of (30) rather than an underlying structure corresponding to that of (29).

Various questions can be raised in connection with this paper. For instance, the question of whether it is advisable to argue that a sentence *x* has the same deep structure grammatically as another sentence *y* 'without proposing what those deep structures are and without proposing any transformational derivations' (p. 24). The least that can be said about such a procedure is that it complicates the discussion considerably.

For my purposes, however, the questions to be raised can be divided into two: (i) Is the difference between the 'accidental' and the 'purposive' sense of sentences like (28) sufficiently argued to conclude that they have syntactically different deep structures? (ii) Is the identity between the sentences (29) and (30) sufficiently argued to conclude that they have the same deep structure?

---

[14] Lakoff's formulation 'the *correct* (italics mine-JGK) generalizations' about selectional restrictions and co-occurrence relations is, however, open to different interpretations.

3.3.1. *Co-occurrence, selection, and synonymy*

With regard to question (i), it should be noted that after having indicated the differences between (28a) and (28b), Lakoff does not pay much attention to the 'accidental' interpretation, and does not suggest a deep structure for it. Since he argues that (28b) does not have a deep structure with a *with*-phrase but a deep structure corresponding to that of (30), it would follow that (28a) also does not have a *with*-phrase in the deep structure. I will return below to the question of the difference between the accidental interpretation (28a) and the purposive interpretation (28b).

With regard to question (ii), it should be noted first of all that Lakott has to discard some other senses of the verb *use*, to make it plausible not only that the sentences *I sliced the salami with a knife* and *I used a knife to slice the salami with* are synonymous, but that in general sentences of the type *use* NP_2 *to V* NP_1 are synonymous with sentences of the type *V* NP_1 *with* NP_2. Thus, the 'generic' sense of *use* in the sentence

(50) The Volkswagen uses disk brakes to provide adequate stopping power

and the 'use-up' sense of *use* in

(51) The contractor used 1000 tons of concrete to build the library

are not considered by Lakoff for the sake of the argument. This already begs an important question, namely, the question of whether the similarity in co-occurrence relations and selectional restrictions between the *with NP*-sentences and the *use NP to*-sentences are not of a lexical rather than a grammatical nature: the contexts that would indicate that these relations and restrictions are grammatical have to be narrowed down considerably[15].

This is especially true of Lakoff's example

(52) The marquis used the knife to please his mother.

This sentence can mean that the marquis succeeded in pleasing his mother with the knife, but it can also mean that he used the knife with that end in view but that it is undecidable whether he did or did not succeed in pleasing her. Such an ambiguity, however, is not present in

(53) The marquis pleased his mother with the knife.

From this, I think, the conclusion can be drawn that one can use the construc-

---

[15] Not to mention the fact that, for some native speakers at least, a sentence like *The contractor built the library with 1000 tons of concrete* is not deviant.

tion *use NP to*, to describe 'some activity for certain purposes' without implying that the desired result or state of affairs was actually achieved, but that
this is not regularly possible when one uses an Instrumental *with NP*-phrase.
Similarly, from the observation made by Lakoff (p. 12 ff.) that (52) can be
interpreted as

(52a) The marquis used the knife in order to please his mother, but he never-
        theless failed to please her

but that (53) cannot be interpreted as

(53a) *The marquis used the knife in order to please his mother, but he never-
        theless failed to please her

one can draw the conclusion that the synonymy between these two types of
sentences is in fact defective and that therefore the proposal that they have
the same deep structure is dubious. What Lakoff does, on the contrary, is to
rule out the 'use-in-order to' sense of *use NP to* as well, until the one sense
of *use* remains by which the synonymy of (29) and (30) can be illustrated.

To this it should be added that Lakoff is well aware of this (p. 25 ff.). It is
his position, that if one followed this line of reasoning, whereby not all conditions of selection and co-occurrence would be equivalent, this would lead
one to doubt one of the most important criteria used for the definition of the
level of deep structure, *viz.* the generalization about selectional restrictions
and co-occurrence relations that can be made by assuming that one sentence
has the same deep structure as another. This, in turn, would entail that one of
the major motivations for having a transformational description could be
dropped as well. Against this, however, the objection can be brought in that
the recognition of the fact that there may be partial identities of selection and
co-occurrence which do not entail identity of grammatical deep structure in
itself, is not an argument against deep structure, or against these criteria, or
against Transformational grammar, for that matter. A grammatical description
that assumes that some sentences in the language are grammatically identical
but not therefore synonymous, or that some other sentences are in some interpretation similar but therefore not identical, is in a position to relegate some
identities to more general conditions of grammatical structure and other identities or differences to less general conditions of lexical structure or even referential plausibility.

Once the criteria such as Lakoff lists in his article, and among which the
criteria of selectional restrictions and co-occurrence loom large, are accepted,
it still remains for the linguist to decide where the boundary has to be drawn
between grammatical identity and interpretational similarity, in order to ob-

tain a description that is balanced between generalization in the description of sets of sentences and adequacy in the description of individual sentences. The theoretical predicament pointed out by Lakoff, only indicates that, whereas identity of selection and co-occurrence is a necessary condition for the fruitful application of concepts like homonymy c.q. synonymy, the reverse is therefore not necessarily true.

Secondly, it can be disputed whether the sentences with *use NP to* and with *with NP*, even under the restriction Lakoff puts on the sense of *use*, are in fact synonymous, in the generally loose sense in which this term is usually applied. This has been denied by Chomsky (unpublished) and I will elaborate on his remarks.

Compare the following pairs of sentences:

(54a) Seymour used this table to write his letter
(54b) ?Seymour wrote his letter with this table
(55a) Seymour used all his intellectual resources to get out of this predicament
(55b) ?Seymour got out of this predicament with all his intellectual resources
(56a) Rodin used a hammer to make this statue
(56b) ?Rodin made this statue with a hammer.

The first pair is not synonymous since (54b) entails that Seymour used his table for a pen, which (54a) does not entail. Even if, with Lakoff, the 'use in order to' sense of (54a) is disregarded, it appears that *use NP to* can imply that something was used in the achievement of a certain goal or the completion of a certain activity where a sentence with *with NP* cannot.

The second pair is not synonymous since the sentence (55b) is hardly acceptable as 'Instrumental'. This indicates that there are restrictions on the NP's that can function as Instrumentals that are different from the restrictions on NP's that can function as Complements to *use*.

The third pair is not synonymous since whereas (56b) implies that the instrument used in making the statue was a hammer, (56a) could also imply that a hammer was only one of the instruments used, or, that it only served as medium of some kind. Thus, I can say

(57a) I used sand to paint this wall

and I can say

(57b) I painted this wall with sand

but sentence (57b) has at least one interpretation with the rather odd implication that I used only sand, whereas (58a) has the quite natural interpretation that I mixed paint and sand to achieve the result wanted. Similarly, the sentences

(58a) Manolito always used his left hand to bring the bull to its knees
(58b) Manolito always brought the bull to its knees with his left hand

certainly can depict two quite different kinds of bullfighters[16]. Notice, furthermore, that the difference between (57a) and (57b) is preserved also when the 'in order to' sense is ruled out, that is, when the sentence is interpreted as 'Resultative'.

These data point to the conclusion that in sentences of the type *use NP to V*, where *use* has the meaning Lakoff concentrates upon, and which describe a completed activity or achieved goal, the NP that serves as Complement to *use*, still can refer to only one of the 'means' applied. It does not necessarily refer to 'the' means by which the activity mentioned was carried out or the state of affairs described was brought about. *Use* has a wider range of application and therefore allows NP's as Complements that *with* does not allow. The non-synonymy of the various *use NP to V* sentences and *V with NP* sentences leads Chomsky (o.c., fn. 16) to the, in my opinion quite plausible, suggestion that the deep structure of a sentence like

(30) I used a knife to slice the salami

is not something like

[I used a knife] [I sliced the salami]

but rather the reverse:

[I sliced the salami] [I used a knife]

with the *use*-phrase as subordinate to the main verb.

On the other hand, there are examples where the alleged synonymy of the sentences with *use NP to* and with *with NP* is suspicious for exactly the opposite reason, *viz.*, because the sentences with *use* are more specific than the sentences with *with*. I would at least feel inclined to doubt the synonymy of the following pairs of sentences, also when the sentences where an Instrumental *with*-phrase occurs are interpreted as 'purposive':

(59a) He hit the man on the jaw with his fist
(59b) ?He used his fist to hit the man on the jaw
(60a) She touched his sleeve with her finger

[16] The man in sentence (58b), in fact, is not a bullfighter but just somebody fighting bulls.

(60b) ?She used her finger to touch his sleeve
(61a) He shocked her with that story
(61b) ?He used that story to shock her.

The unnaturalness of the second sentence of each pair corresponds to the fact that *use* emphasizes the activity described, and that it furthermore suggests an actual 'choice' of means. It is precisely one of the features of the Instrumental *with*-phrases that they leave the exact nature of the activity implicit by not mentioning it, and that no 'choice' of means is suggested at all. The natural paraphrase of a sentence like (61a) is

> 'He shocked her by telling her that story'

and not

> 'He used that story in shocking her'.

3.3.2. *The notion 'Instrumental'*

It seems there is some real confusion here over the scope of the term 'Instrumental'.

Let us assume that among the grammatical functions to be distinguished in English sentences there is a function 'Instrumental'. Let us also assume that the preposition usually connected with Instrumental prepositional phrases is *with*. Then, we have such sentences as

(62) The car hit the kerb with its right wheel
(60a) She touched his sleeve with her finger
(1) He hit the man with the stick
(29) I sliced the salami with a knife
(28) I cut my finger with a knife
(63) He delighted the king with gifts from abroad
(64) He succeeded in calming down the assembly with a few well-spoken words
(65) He succeeded in breaking the window with a tyre-iron
(61a) He shocked her with that story
(66) He stuffed their minds with fuzzy issues

What the prepositional phrases in all these sentences have in common is that they point to the 'means' by which some activity described is carried out or some state of affairs described is brought about[17]. What can also be seen from

---

[17] In Fillmore's formulation (1968:24) 'the case of the inanimate force or object causally involved in the action or state identified by the verb'. 'Causally involved' is a bit vague, another problem – see below, p. 114-5 – is the restriction 'Inanimate'.

the above examples, is that the notion 'Instrumental' ranges over a variety of such means, from concrete 'instruments' to not so concrete 'means' or 'activities'; in the total structure of the sentence, the rôle of the prepositional *with*-phrases is basically the same. This, I would say, is precisely one of the reasons for regarding them as representing one and the same grammatical function. In fact, one of Lakoff's own examples is the sentence

(67) Paul analyzed the English passive construction with himself as an informant

which is rather an abstract instance of an 'Instrumental' relation, and on closer inspection seems to be much nearer to a prepositional phrase of mere 'Circumstance'. Compare

(68) Paul staged Hamlet with himself as Polonius.

But, as said before, making distinctions will imply borderline cases.

In any case, a variety of 'entities' or 'forces' as Fillmore defines it, can be involved instrumentally in a variety of activities or states of affairs brought about. Therefore, there will always be interpretational differences between sentences with Instrumental *with*-phrases, for instance between sentences like (28) and (29), (1) and (60a), (64) and (65). The question is whether these differences lead to the conclusion that the sentences concerned do not have the same grammatical structure, and what consequences that conclusion would have for their grammatical description as well as for the description of the grammatical structure of other sentences.

This brings us back to question (i), the question of whether the difference between the 'accidental' and 'purposive' interpretation of (28) is indeed a reflection of a deep-structure grammatical difference. Consider again

(28a) I cut my finger with a knife (accidental)
(28b) I cut my finger with a knife (purposive).

As noted earlier, Lakoff does not propose a deep structure for the accidental interpretation. Whatever it looks like, it must certainly indicate that under both interpretations the NP in the *with*-phrase is the 'inanimate entity' which brings about the described result. Under both interpretations of (28), the cut in the finger is made by a knife, whether it happened accidentally or was done on purpose. This would at least suggest that the two interpretations of this sentence are quite close as far as basic grammatical relations are concerned. For instance, if the underlying structure was assumed to be something like

[I had a knife] [I cut my finger]
[I was with a knife] [I cut my finger]

this would fail to account for the interpretational feature 'instrument'. It is true, that *use NP to* is inappropriate to a paraphrase the 'accidental' interpretation, but in itself this proves very little — the more so since *use* is also inappropriate to paraphrase some of the non-accidental interpretations, as we saw.

But rather than guessing what the deep structure of (28a) would be, it might be worth while to investigate the conditions under which *both* the accidental *and* the purposive interpretations are possible.

Compare

(69a) He cut his finger with a knife
(70a) He hit a pedestrian with the rear of his car

and

(69b) He cut his finger
(70b) He hit a pedestrian.

Since the accidental and the purposive interpretation are possible in both sets of sentences, this ambiguity apparently has little to do with the Instrumental *with*-phrases themselves. It appears, on the contrary, that the possibility of an accidental interpretation is largely dependent from aspectual features expressed in the Verb Phrase and lexical features of the Verbs.

As for the first point, it possibly is not a coincidence that all Lakoff's examples are in the Past Tense, since the accidental interpretation is connected most naturally with a 'completed activity'.

As for the second point, compare the sentences

(71) He broke the vase
(72) He painted the vase.

There is an accidental and purposive interpretation of (71), but there hardly is an accidental interpretation of (72). I do not doubt that the difference between 'accidental' and 'purposive' is relevant in the description of English sentences, but I do doubt whether it is a difference deserving such emphasis in the discussion of Instrumental Adverbs as a category. It should be recalled here that the argument that (29) and (30) are 'same' hinges on the argument that (28a) and (28b) are 'different', since otherwise the synonymy of (29) and (30) breaks down.

Another argument against the assumption that we have a basic distinction here is the fact that there are examples where neither an 'accidental' nor a 'purposive' interpretation is very appropriate. Consider sentences like

(73) He really brought the house down with his second piano solo
(74) They frightened him with their stoicism
(75) He delighted the king with gifts from abroad
(76) Darwin shocked Christian Europe with his theories

In all four examples, the interpretation is that X affects Y, or brings about some state of Y, 'with' Z. It is difficult to imagine, however, that the means that bring about the described state of affairs are applied 'with that purpose' in any relevant sense of the term, since what finally happens is not a foreseeable consequence of what the Subject of the sentence does. On the other hand, the 'accidental' sense like we have in (28) 'I cut my finger on a knife' is also not the first interpretation one thinks of in connection with these sentences.

Take the example of (74). One quite natural interpretation of this sentence is that the stoic behaviour of some people in some situation caused some person to become frightened. Hence the paraphrase

(74a) Their stoicism frightened him

This is not 'purposive' since it is not implied by (74) that 'their' behaviour was meant to frighten 'him'. Nor is it accidental in the sense that you use a knife for some purpose and as a result get your finger cut. What Lakoff calls 'accidental' might better be labelled 'non-intentional', therefore. This, however, still does not solve the problem. A sentence like (75) does not imply that somebody was intentionally or willfully delighted with gifts. With verbs like *shock, delight, frighten,* such an interpretation is unnatural and if one wants to imply it, one will use adverbs like *deliberately*. On the other hand, an accidental interpretation is also somewhat unnatural: one does not present somebody with gifts *not* to delight him in the way one uses a knife for cutting bread and not for getting one's finger cut. I would say that a sentence like (76) illustrates that Instrumental *with*-phrases can be completely neutral in this respect.

The same problem arises with sentences without such phrases. There is an 'intentional' and a 'non-intentional' interpretation of

(69b) He cut his finger

but when one tries to decide whether the one interpretation, or the other interpretation, or maybe both, hold in a sentence like

(77) They frightened him

things become rather cloudy.

One can object that perhaps neither 'purposive' vs. 'accidental' nor 'intentional' vs. 'non-intentional' are appropriate labels to indicate the differences, or that there are three or four ambiguities in such sentences rather than two. The opposite conclusion is more plausible in my opinion: there may be a variety of ambiguities or nuances in these sentences, and the difference between intentional and non-intentional is certainly relevant for many sentences and lexical elements, but that does not split up Instrumental *with*-phrases into two categories. To return once more to the original example, besides

(78a) John sliced the salami with a knife

and

(78b) John cut his finger with a knife

we have a sentence like

(78c) John spoiled the salami with a knife

which can be paraphrased as 'John did do something to the salami with a knife with· the result that the salami was spoilt'. It is immaterial here, or rather, it depends on contextual features that the sentence does not provide, whether John did this on purpose − he might be one of those people −, or whether he did it accidentally − he might be honest but clumsy − or whether the question simply does not arise.

3.3.3. *Syntactic or semantic categories*?

Semantic intuitions, however, do not settle the issue. I will therefore add some comments on the grammatical contexts listed by Lakoff˙− examples (31) to (35) above − where the accidental interpretation of a sentence like (28) is ruled out. It should be recalled that what is at stake here is the level of deep structure where (Lakoff o.c. p. 4) grammatical relations such as [Subject of] , [Object of] , are defined in terms of the fundamental categories of phrase structure.

(a) (31) I was cutting my finger with a knife.

The non-intentional interpretation conflicts with the Aspectual feature Progressive. This is true, but at least for some native speakers it is not true for the sentence

(31a) I was cutting my finger with the knife.

The point is, then, whether this constraint entails a deep structure difference in terms of grammatical categories. One other reason to doubt this is that there are other 'non-intentional' sentences where the constraint does not work:

(31b) You are suffocating me with your strong arms
(31c) She was causing uproar with her new dress
(31d) You are killing yourself with all those cigarettes

(b) (32) I cut my finger without a knife.

The phrase *without a knife* rules out the accidental interpretation of *I cut my finger*. This may be true, but I must admit that I am at a loss to see the relevance of this example. Substituting *without* for *with* rules out the Instrumental interpretation entirely, and that also happens in 'intentional' sentences. Compare

(32a) He scored that goal with his left foot
(32b) ?He scored that goal without his left foot

(c) (33) Cut your finger with a knife.

The accidental interpretation conflicts with the Imperative. One does not command the involuntary result of an activity. As in the case of (31), I doubt whether this generalization is syntactic. Adding the feature [+Neg] , for instance, removes the constraint, since one can say

(33a) Don't hurt yourself with that knife

(d) (34) I carefully cut my finger with a knife.

The presence of the adverb *carefully* rules out the interpretation 'accidental'. Similarly, the adverb *inadvertently* rules out the interpretation 'intentional'. The limits of expediency of such a line of reasoning are reached when we observe that *on purpose* rules out the 'accidental' interpretation and *by accident* the 'purposive' interpretation. So, some adverbs will reinforce one possible interpretation of a sentence, and other adverbs will reinforce another possible interpretation, and others will still not resolve the ambiguity such as *certainly*, and yet other adverbs will make the sentence odd, such as *respectfully*.

What in general is confusing about Lakoff's arguments is that they are used as arguments against the assumption that (28a) and (28b) have the same deep structure in terms of basic grammatical relations. I would say that on the contrary the contexts adduced explain implicitly the difference between primary syntactic categories and secondary syntactic categories, and between the grammatical structure of a sentence and its meaning. It is, in particular, clear that the 'accidental' interpretation of sentences such as (28) depends on various features of grammatical and sometimes lexical structure that therefore do not affect the argument that the two interpretations have the same syntactic structure. In fact, if 'having the same syntactic structure' is equated with 'being capable of co-occurring with the same elements in the same string', the concept loses its significance.

The same applies in the reverse for the examples (36) to (49), which in my opinion only show that some sentences, without being syntactically identical, can, under proper circumstances, have the same meaning, and that this of course entails that they obey certain restrictions of selection and co-occurrence. As we have seen above, there are other contexts where the difference between sentences with *with NP* and *use NP to* is quite clear, which furthermore point to the conclusion that their syntactic identity is dubious and that semantically there are arguments against viewing *use* as the Main Verb. It is for instance an equivocation to state that since in both (42) and (43) the NP that functions as Subject has the categorial restriction 'NP must be Animate' (p.73), this is an argument in favour of the syntactic identity of these two sentences. This is essentially the kind of argument by which it can be proved that Verbs and Adjectives are the 'same' category since there are sets of Verbs and sets of Adjectives that share the feature (-Stative) vs. (+Stative). There are other features that they certainly do not share, and as long as that is the case the argument is indeterminate[18]. The pairs of sentences

(40a) John killed Harry
(40b) Harry was killed by John
(42a) The explosion killed Harry
(42b) Harry was killed by the explosion

are 'same' in terms of the traditional notions Subject-Predicate-Object, but that does not entail, in reverse that they are not also fundamentally different on another level, since *John* and *The explosion* are categorically distinguished as (+Animate) vs. (-Animate).

Finally, some comments are in order on the examples (48) and (49). Lakoff convincingly argues that in both sentences, *slice the salami* cannot be

---

[18] I have similar misgivings about Lyons' remark (1968:397 ff.) that significant generalizations would be lost if verbs like *come* and *go* were to be regarded as deep structure verbs. According to Lyons, the sentences *John comes to San Francisco* and *John goes to San Francisco* both express a dynamic relationship, as compared to *John is in San Francisco*; the differences between *come* and *go* can be explained by regarding these verbs as realizations of the semantic features 'proximity' and 'remoteness' respectively. This in itself is not objectionable, but why should elements like *come* and *go* stop being verbs as soon as it can be pointed out that they share features with *here* and *there*, or *to* and *from*? Besides, the structure of *come* and *go* is much more complicated; see Fillmore (1966).

negated, since (p. 19) 'One cannot use an instrument in an action that does
not occur' (though this should be rather phrased as: one cannot take *with
the knife* as Instrumental in this sentence).

   Lakoff argues that this can syntactically be formulated as a constraint
that the Complement of *use* cannot be negated, just as other Verb Comple-
mentizers cannot be negated. According to him, such a constraint cannot be
stated under the assumption that the deep structure of

(29) I sliced the salami with a knife

is something like

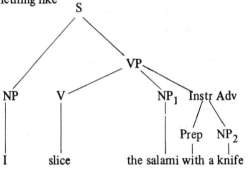

In that configuration, *slice the salami* would not be a VP in itself; it would
not even be a constituent, and on the other hand, the Instrumental prepositional phrase would be part of the VP. Other arguments for regarding VP's as
constituents in sentences with Manner Adverbs or Instrumental Adverbs adduced by Lakoff are the similarities between sentences like

(79) Max gives girls books and Benny does so too
(80) Max slices salami with a knife and Benny does so with a cleaver.

But if the observations on the VP in the above sentences are correct and hold
good for other sentences as well, the first thing that springs to mind, I would
say, is to consider that the formalism might need revision, and to change it accordingly:

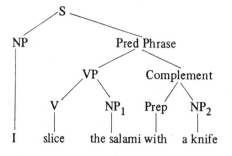

In this way, we introduce Adverbial Complements of Manner and Instrument as optional Complements to the VP in the Predicate Phrase, just as Complements of Time and Place are optionally introduced as Complements to the Predicate Phrase. We then are able to state the possibilities of and constraints on Topicalization and Negation: the whole sentence can be negated, or the VP, or the Instrumental Adverb ('it was not with a knife that I sliced the salami'). But when the Instrumental Adverb is topicalized, the VP cannot be negated. Again, I cannot see why it is imperative to assume that the syntactic deep structure must be that of the construction *use NP$_2$ to V NP$_1$*.

3.4. Concluding remarks

Summarizing, interpretational and distributional data as adduced by Lakoff for (28) can only be used to argue for or against identity of grammatical deep structure, if it can also be argued that the grammatical description improves. As far as the Instrumental *with*-phrases discussed in this section are concerned, I must say that I doubt this very much. To make it plausible that two sentences *x* and *y* do not have the same grammatical structure C it is necessary to argue that *x* belongs to a set of sentences that has the grammatical structure A and that *y* belongs to a set of sentences that has the grammatical structure B, and that these two grammatical structures are different. In my opinion, the foregoing discussion points on the contrary to the conclusion that (i) the 'accidental' and 'purposive' Instrumental sentences have the same grammatical structure as far as the notion Instrumental is concerned, and that their ambiguity is an ambiguity of an entirely different nature that is furthermore not even diacritic for these sentences since there are others that have neither an accidental nor purposive interpretation. (ii) That it is as difficult, if not far more difficult, to sustain the identity between the *with NP* and the *use NP to* sentences. (iii) That in both cases what is gained in generalization in terms of co-occurrence and selectional restrictions on the one hand is lost in adequacy and generalization of identity of grammatical relations on the other hand.

The latter point may be dwelt upon a little longer. The purpose of the application of such 'functional' labels as Instrumental, is to obtain a form of generalization about the relations between constituents in a sentence, or, if one wants, about the semantic rôle that constituents have in the structure of a sentence despite their mutual differences[19]. Such a description proceeds from the tacit or explicit assumption that these generalizations are needed at some level of the description of sentences, for essentially the same reasons as the well-known generalizations about constituent structure are needed: to relate sentence structures despite their mutual differences. A label like Prepositional Phrase covers different categories of prepositional phrases, just as a label like Adverb covers different constituents; adverbs and prepositional phrases. By the same token, different Instrumental relations can be subsumed under the label Instrumental. To prove that such a generalization is unsuitable for the purpose of a linguistic description — or, to prove that the level of description at which these generalizations are made is in itself insignificant[20] — one will have to prove either that a more significant generalization can be obtained at this level, or that the generalizations should be made on another, more 'abstract' level (Lakoff p. 24). I maintain that Lakoff's article does not prove either of these two things, within the reasonable limits one may set to the notion 'proof' in a linguistic discussion. The synonymy of the *with NP* sentences and the *use NP to* sentences is not convincingly argued, and no actual alternative or more abstract deep structures are proposed. I maintain, on the contrary, that his article *does* indicate that in order to prove that a grammatical description of a sentence is inadequate it certainly is not sufficient to point out that not all ambiguities are accounted for at one and the same level.

---

[19] As put forward for instance in Fillmore's case grammar.

[20] This appears to be at least a consequence Lakoff reckons with, if not (yet) his ultimate goal. In this respect, his article marks the transition from generative syntax to generative semantics.

4. AMBIGUITY AND GRAMMAR: THE PROBLEM OF NEUTRA-LIZATION

4.1. Relatedness and equivalence

The observations made in the foregoing chapter are not meant as a belated defence of the notion 'Gesamtbedeutung'. They are intended to bring to attention some of the problems that arise from the diacritical use of the notion ambiguity in grammatical description, and in linguistic description in general. What I want to underline in particular is the fact that if one argues that the structure of a sentence, or part of its structure, is in fact closely related to the structure or part of the structure of another sentence, ohe should also try to show how far the grammatical equivalence of these structures extends. This problem poses itself most prominently with sentences that are viewed as being homonymous in the sense that they represent more than one grammatical structure, but it does present itself elsewhere too.

Thus, it has been observed by various authors that the Adnominal *with*-phrases in sentences like

(1) The girl with the flowers is my niece
(2) A bull with real courage is sometimes less dangerous
(3) He hit the man with the stick

are semantically or 'notionally' related to expressions with *have* in the general sense of 'being with' or 'having some relation with'. This observation can be extended, as it is by Lyons (1968: 391 ff.), to the categories of 'Possession', 'Existence', and 'Location'[1]. Compare

(4a) The list has six names on it
(4b) The six names on the list
(5a) The book is John's
(5b) John's book
(6a) The book is on the table
(6b) The book on the table

The latter proposal derives some additional plausibility from the fact that

---

[1] For a semantic analysis of the various functions of *have*, see Bendix (1966:37 ff.).

there are languages where the relatedness of these categories on the level of grammatical constructions is quite conspicuous (see e.g. Lyons 1968: 393), for instance, where the same construction indicates 'Location' with some Nouns and 'Possession' with other Nouns. Thus, we can say that the sentence

(7) He saw the man with the camera

is equivalent to an underlying structure that can be represented roughly as

(7) [He saw the man] [the man $\left\{\begin{matrix} \text{have} \\ \text{be with} \end{matrix}\right\}$ camera]

Furthermore, Adnominal Complements can be either Restrictive or Appositive. This can be indicated in the constituent structure by developing the *with*-phrase either as a Complement *within* the NP — possibly as an extension of the (+ Def) determiner — or as Complement *to* the NP². This would explain the ambiguity of sentences like

(8a) He found the man with the camera
(9a) He saw the man with the stick

where the prepositional phrase can be interpreted as Restrictive or as Appositive. In the first interpretation, we have the structure of

(8b) The man with the camera was found
(9b) The man with the stick was seen

and in the second interpretation we have the structure of

(8c) The man was found, with the camera
(9c) The man was seen, with the stick

In itself, then, the observation that the *with*-phrases in these sentences are realizations of a more general category that can be labelled 'have' for short, is no less plausible than that all Adverbial *with*-phrases basically share a feature 'Circumstance'. The point is, however, at what level of description do such observations become relevant.

In *Aspects*, (1965:102 ff.), Chomsky tentatively suggests that some of the prepositional phrases usually labelled 'Manner Adverbials' are in fact to be viewed as transforms of Adnominal Complements to the Subject, e.g.

---

² See Smith (1964), Chomsky (1965:100), and fn. 26. Schwartz (1968) proposes a modification of the base rules by which the relatedness between the two types of complements would be preserved. One problem inherent in their separate generation is that, semantically, the distinction 'Restrictive' vs. 'Appositive' is less clear in many contexts with indefinite noun phrases than with definite noun phrases.

(10a) [John $\begin{Bmatrix} \text{have} \\ \text{be with} \end{Bmatrix}$ enthusiasm] [John read the book]

(10b) John read the book with enthusiasm

The Transformational rules, however, that finally give (10b) from (10a) will have to indicate that there is a considerable change in syntactic relations at the level of the sentence. The Adverbial Phrase *with enthusiasm* is no longer related to the Subject, but to the activity described in the Verb Phrase, or rather to both. Besides Complements that can be viewed essentially as Modifiers to the Subject, there are others that are essentially to be viewed as modifications of the relation Subject-Verb Phrase. This difference appears from sentences like

(11)   John read the book with a flower in his ear

(12)   John read the book with enthusiasm

where we have

(11a) I saw John with a flower in his ear

but not

(12a) *I saw John with enthusiasm

though we do have

(11b) I saw John reading the book with a flower in his ear

and

(12b) I saw John reading the book with enthusiasm

That some Complements to the Subject function as Manner Adverbials at the sentence level could be explained in a description that allows for the introduction of basic syntactic features alongside the basic category symbols. In the course of the derivation, these features would change the function of the Complements, or alternatively, specify them for those functional distinctions regarding which they are neutral at a higher level. In a Transformational description, where, at least as far as basic grammatical relations are concerned, transformations are supposed to be meaning preserving, there is a major problem here. In itself, the transformation that brings the original Nominal Subject Complement under the scope of the Verb Phrase does not explain its function in the sentence. The difference between Manner Adverbials and Adnominal Complements at the sentence level cuts across their possible deep structure similarity, which is a reason for regarding Manner Adverbials as primitives of the syntactic structure of such sentences, and not as derived from allegedly more fundamental deep structure configurations. The same would, a fortiori, be true of Instrumentals: a deep structure like

(13) [John $\begin{Bmatrix} \text{have} \\ \text{be with} \end{Bmatrix}$ stone] [John attacked the policeman]

would transform to *John attacked the policeman with a stone in his hand*, and not necessarily to *John attacked the policeman with a stone*, unless, again, one assumes that a feature 'Instrument' is introduced at the sentence level[3].

A grammatical description, therefore, will have to achieve some balance between on the one hand, the recognition that structures that are different at the sentence level, might be related at a deeper level, and on the other hand, the recognition of the fact that such deep structure similarities are mainly semantic or notional[4], and have been 'recategorized' — to use another term of Lyons' — at the sentence level to the extent that the mutual differences of the two structures become no less crucial than their similarities. If some such notion as 'recategorization' is not taken into account, the problem arises that, either different structures that are viewed as same are only partially equivalent, or that their equivalence has to be explained by pointing out some very general or vague feature they share. But then, the problems connected with the notion 'Gesamtbedeutung' which one tries to get rid of by relating a structure *x* to other structures, creep in again by the backdoor. In those cases where a grammatical structure *x* is regarded as homonymous, in the sense that it represents a structure *y* and a structure *z*, one will have the same problem multiplied.

In point of fact, the notion 'recategorization' does not leave the Instrumental category unaffected either. Fillmore states (1968:32) that the preposition usually connected with the Instrumental category is *with*, and that it is *by* when there is no Agent. Compare

(14a) He was killed by Harry with a knife
(14b) He was killed by a knife

(see also Lyons 1968:297-8). However, from a sentence like

---

[3] Compare Schwartz (1968:749): 'What is a bit unsettling is the idea that there are kinds of relatedness within the power of a transformational rule which go deeper than synonymy, that there are primitive structural configurations whose semantic reflexes will be, almost of necessity, startingly diverse'. For a related criticism of the base rules that introduce Manner Adverbs and Instrumental Adverbs see Fillmore (1969: 361 ff.).
[4] This is also the conclusion drawn in Bendix (1966).

(15) He was killed by a stray bullet

one might wonder to what extent such a generalization can be extended. The sentence (15) does not necessarily have the implication that there is an implicit (+Animate) Agent; the message conveyed is rather that some Inanimate force is regarded as 'Cause'. In fact, sentence (15) is as close to (14a) as it is to the sentences

(16) He was hit by the bucket of a dragline
(17) The village was destroyed by the flood

where we also have

(16a) The bucket of a dragline hit him
(17a) The flood destroyed the village

But beside the sentence

(18) The book was written with a golden pen

we hardly have

(18a) ?The book was written by a golden pen
(18b) ?A golden pen wrote the book

or at least, only in a metaphorical sense. This would indicate that there are Inanimate entities that are 'Agentive' rather than 'Instrumental'; the sentences (16a) and (17a) are certainly not equivalent in this respect to Fillmore's example of an Instrumental as Subject (1968: 25):

(19) The key opened the door

If one wants to restrict the use of the term Agentive to [+Animate] Nouns, the conclusion would have to be that there are cases where the distinction between the syntactic functions of [+Animate] and [−Animate] Nouns is grammatically 'neutralized', in the positive sense of 'not being relevant' when these Nouns are Subjects in either Active or Passive constructions.

4.1.1. *Ambiguity, neutrality and vagueness*

Thus far, I have tried to demonstrate that the ambiguity criterion in grammatical description does not apply as easily as it might seem to[5]. Nominalizations as in the nominal *with*-phrases are a case in point here, since they are connected with the ambiguity problem in several ways. Compared to the

---

[5] For footnote, see next page.

verbal structures they can be related to, many nominalizations have the
notorious property that they only partially share the features of verbal expressions, for instance, they are only very defectively specified for the typical
verbal features such as Tense and Aspect, and that furthermore they may
have additional features the verbal structures do not have[6].

Another problem entailed by the derivation of nominal constructions from
verbal constructions is that of the choice of an underlying verb. Often, choice
of an underlying verb is arbitrary with respect to the interpretational possibilities the nominalized expressions allow for. This is most conspicuously a
feature of Lees' syntactic analysis of English compounds (Lees 1966[4]). The
difficulty, of course, can be remedied by pushing the diversity of underlying
and derived structures back step by step till an abstract underlying structure
remains that is suitable for the purposes of the derivational approach. But
this poses the question of whether, once this procedure is followed, it is in
fact not more expedient to regard a nominal structure A and a verbal structure B as different realizations of the same basic relation, rather than assuming that one of them is derived from the structure underlying the other[7].

In what follows, I will illustrate only some of the problems that arise in
the description of Nominal constructions as 'derivatives'. I will, furthermore,
approach these problems primarily from the point of view of semantic adequacy.

4.1.1.1. *Nominalizations and the feature 'Tense'*
Nominal expressions have the typical property that they are not specified
for the features Tense and Aspect of comparable Verbal structures. This can,
in principle, be accounted for in two ways. The one way is to assume that the
Nominal expressions are inherently ambiguous in the sense that they 'have'
the Tense and Aspect features of an underlying verbal structure, but that these

---

[5] I claim no originality for this observation. As early as 1961, Bolinger convincingly
demonstrated that Transformational grammar tends to focus its attention on the clear-cut
cases of 'diversification' and to overlook the more complicated cases of syntactic blends.
See his comments on Lees (1960) in Bolinger (1961c).

[6] The problems with the transformational derivation of nominalizations of the type
John's sincerity have been treated extensively in Chomsky (1970). For an analysis of
the ambiguity between a 'Factive' and a 'Manner' sense of gerundials of the type *John's
cooking*, see Wonder (1970).

[7] The traditional objection against such an approach is that it entails redundancy:
however, when the diversity between two related structures is about as great as their
identity, this objection loses much of its force.

features are not overtly expressed. The second way is to assume that they are not inherently ambiguous between the various features of Tense and Aspect of the verbal structures, but that they are inherently unspecified in these respects.

The problem with the first approach is that there are quite severe restrictions on the ways in which Nominal expressions can be interpreted. Thus, the Adnominal Complement *with the camera* in

(20) He hit the man with the camera

can be interpreted as, say,

(20a) He hit the man who carried the camera

but it cannot be interpreted as, for instance,

(20c) *He hit the man who might have carried the camera

(compare Bach 1968:98 ff.). That is, of the various realizations of the Aux element in the underlying structure which serves as a cover term for Aspectual and Tense features, only some are possible in the Nominalization. This can be accounted for by saying that a nominal expression as *the man with the camera* cannot be Counterfactual or Hypothetical, or, that the possibilities of the Verbal constructions are in fact reduced to two: +Positive (*the man with the camera*) or −Positive (*the man without the camera*)[8] and that in the case of sentence (20) the only possibility is Positive, or Factual.

What remains, however, is that (20) above can still be interpreted as

(20a) He hit the man who *carried* the camera

or as

(20b) He hit the man who *carries* a camera.

Also in a sentence like

(21) He looked at the girl with the red hair

there are two possible interpretations. Either, the girl with the red hair is the girl who 'then' had red hair, i.e. the THEN girl with red hair, or the Noun Phrase refers to a girl who 'now' has red hair, i.e. the NOW girl with red hair.

Assuming that the Nominal expression is related to, or derived from an abstract underlying verbal structure, with no actual main verb but only a verbal

---

[8] To which should be added that *without*-phrases correspond only very defectively to *with*-phrases.

element Aux, one can, with Bach (ibid.) assume that in this underlying structure the Nominal expression has two different Tense elements: a 'Narrative
Tense' and a 'True Present'. The Narrative Tense is a Tense feature that assumes the value of the context of the sentence:

(22a) He *saw* the man who *carried* a camera
(23a) He *sees* the man who *carries* a camera

and the True Present is a Tense element that remains invariable in context:

(22b) He *saw* the man who *carries* a camera
(23b) He *sees* the man who *carries* a camera

This reduces the inherent ambiguity of the Nominalization, as far as the
Tense element is concerned, to a two-way one. To this it should be added that
assuming such an element as 'Narrative Tense' is in fact tantamount to recognizing that, in comparison with the verbal structures, the Nominal expression
is unspecified with respect to the feature Tense.

There are, however, reasons for assuming that even this quite fundamental
reduction of the inherent ambiguity of the nominal expression is still not
adequate enough to explain the interpretational possibilities and restrictions.

To quote one of Bach's examples in a slightly altered shape, it is true that
a sentence like

(25) The Russians will put a well-trained man on the moon

can be interpreted as 'The Russian will put a man on the moon who is THEN
well trained', or, that *a well-trained man* can, but does not have to refer to a
man who is NOW well-trained. This can be explained by assuming that in the
first interpretation the Tense element is Narrative, but in the interpretation
'The Russians will put a man on the moon who is NOW well-trained', equivalent to 'The man the Russians will put on the moon is well-trained', the
Tense element is the True Present[9]. However, in Noun Phrases where both
Determiners are (+Definite), this does not work. We have

(22) He saw the man with the camera
(23) He sees the man with the camera
(24) You will see the man with the camera tomorrow

but if *with the camera* is a Restrictive Complement, the latter sentence does
not mean 'you will see the man who will carry a camera' but it means 'you
will see the NOW man with the camera'. Similarly, the sentence,

[9] 'Present' might still be ambiguous between 'general' and 'temporal', but I will leave
this complication out of consideration.

(26) Tomorrow we will have to talk to the girl with the red hair

does not refer to a girl that THEN has red hair, but can only be interpreted in the sense that reference is made to some NOW girl with red hair.

To formulate it more precisely, the presupposition connected with sentences (24) and (26) is that the Noun Phrases refer to somebody already spoken about; therefore, the relation between the Head Noun and its Adjunct is presupposed to have been already established and is not interpreted as a relation to be established in the future. This latter interpretation would be possible if the Complement were taken as Appositive, but not if it were taken as Restrictive. Compare:

(24a) The man with the camera will be there tomorrow
(24b) The man will be there tomorrow, with the camera

Thus, the assumption that there is a 'Narrative' Tense in the underlying structure of Nominal expressions which takes the value of the Tense element of the context of the sentence, only explains some interpretations. There are others that are not explained by it.

In my opinion, this distinction made between 'True Present' and 'Narrative', to account for the ambiguity of sentences like *he saw the man with the camera*, or, *he saw the girl with the red hair*, can be explained more readily in the following way.

Nominal expressions of this kind, that is, Noun Phrases with a nominal Adjunct, can refer either to the TIME 'spoken about' or to the TIME 'spoken at'. It is these features of the sentences in which they occur *and* of the discourse that determine their interpretation, rather than an underlying ambiguous Tense element of the Nominalizations themselves.

We can assume that in any sentence there is a TIME 'spoken about', for instance, PAST in (22), and a TIME 'spoken at'. The latter can be referred to as NOW for short, standing for 'the TIME of the situation surrounding the utterance token'. Assuming furthermore that for the three sentences (22), (23), and (24) the TIME spoken at is NOW, the TIME spoken at in sentence (22) and in (24) is distinct from the TIME spoken about; the TIME of the discourse surrounding the utterance token is distinct from the TIME referred to in the sentence. In sentence (23), however, they are identical. Hence, (23) can be interpreted only as 'He sees the man who NOW *carries* a camera'; it cannot be interpreted as 'He sees the man who *will* carry a camera', or as 'He sees the man who *carried* a camera'. The combination of the elements PRES and *with the camera* implies that the relation between the man and the camera is Factual

NOW. The sentence (22), however, can be interpreted as 'He saw the man who NOW, at the time spoken at, carries a camera', or it can be interpreted as 'the man who, at the time spoken about, carries a camera', which gives 'the man who THEN *carried* a camera'. The Nominalization itself, then, can be left un-specified for 'Tense'. It is transparent with respect to the TIME elements of the context in which it is embedded, and accordingly takes the value either of the sentence in which it occurs, or of the discourse, or, in some cases, of both. Assuming that all sentences have a feature TIME 'spoken about' that is re-alized by the Tense element of the Verb, and that a feature TIME 'spoken at' is by definition implied in all sentences of a natural language, the difference between (22) and (23) can, schematically, be represented as follows

(22) $Pres_D$ [Past [He SEE] [+Def MAN with CAMERA]]
(23) $Pres_D$ [Pres [He SEE] [+Def MAN with CAMERA]]

where the subscript 'D' for Discourse refers to TIME 'spoken at'.

In both sentences, either the TIME feature of the sentence as an utterance, or the TIME feature of the Verb, can be distributed to the Noun Phrase. In (22) this gives two different interpretations, but in (23) the result is the same.

There is one more reason that argues in favour of this approach. This is the fact that the distinction between the 'Narrative Tense' and 'True Present' appears to be less relevant with (−Def) Determiners. Compare the sentences

(27a) He saw a girl with a white hat
(27b) He sees a girl with a white hat
(27c) He will see a girl with a white hat

It would appear that the possibility of interpreting the first sentence as 'He saw a THEN girl who NOW wears a white hat', does not exist. Of course, it may very well be that the girl referred to is now walking around with a white hat, but this is not something which can be inferred from that sentence, as it can in

(27d) He saw the girl with the white hat

Apparently, in the case of an Indefinite Noun Phrase, paraphrasable as

Some [GIRL with WHITE HAT]

the Noun Phrase will automatically be taken to have the same Tense value as the sentence in which it occurs: NOW in (27b) and NOT NOW in (27a) and (27c). Hence the interpretations:

(27a) He saw a girl who THEN had a white hat
(27b) He sees a girl who NOW has a white hat
(27c) He will see a girl who THEN has a white hat

All three imply that the relation between the Noun and its Complement is a function of the TIME spoken about in the sentence itself, and not of the discourse outside the sentence, or, the TIME spoken at.

This can be explained by the difference between the determiners. A (+Def) determiner makes the Noun Phrase refer to 'some contextually definite person', where the context can either be the TIME spoken about or the TIME spoken at. But since the Determiner is (+Def), the relation between the Noun and its Complement is also taken to be Factual, and not Hypothetical. Therefore, in sentences with a Future like (24) and (26) and with a (+Def) Noun Phrase, the relation between the Noun and its Complement does not refer to the future TIME spoken about. It must refer to an actual situation, that is, to the TIME spoken at. On the other hand, when the Determiner is (−Def), the Noun Phrase only refers to 'some person'. The relation between the Noun and its Complement can accordingly only refer to the TIME of the context of the sentence itself, and not to the TIME of any context outside the sentence, that is, to the situation at the TIME spoken at[10].

This solution, which takes the neutral or unspecified approach to the problem of the Tense element in Noun Phrases, has the advantage that it can explain both the differences and the similarities between (+Def) and (−Def) Noun Phrases with regard to this feature, and that the interpretational possibilities connected with the relation between 'situation at the time spoken about' and 'situation at the time spoken at' are explained in a uniform manner.

4.1.1.2. *Nominalizations and underlying verbs*

Another problem with the derivational approach to Nominalizations is the choice of an underlying verb, which entails difficulties both of semantic adequacy and recoverability of deletion.

We could assume, in Noun Phrases like *the man with the camera*, that the underlying verb is 'carry'. This, of course, would be quite arbitrary, since the man might as well be working with the camera, and if he carries it he might carry it in his hand or on his back, so that 'carry' itself is vague. This problem can be avoided by assuming that the underlying verb is 'have', or, that the relation expressed is no more definite than the relation expressed by the verb *have*.

---

[10] This is another instance where the feature (+Def) plays a crucial role.

But this implies that the various interpretations of the relation between MAN and CAMERA expressed in the phrase *the man with the camera*, are not *definable* ambiguities, but that these various interpretations can only be roughly indicated, for instance, by assuming that the relation expressed is either 'some accidental' relation or 'some inherent' relation. The exact interpretation will depend on the lexical elements involved, and on speakers' imaginative capabilities.

The same, in fact, applies to another realization of the notion 'have', the so-called adnominal possessive in sentences like

(28) John's books are on the table
(29) My books are on the table

Whenever the adnominal possessive is not unambiguously interpretable as 'Subjective' or 'Objective' genitive, as it is for instance in

(30) John's assassination (of x)
(31) John's assassination (by x)

the interpretational possibilities increase proportionally[11]. *John's books* can mean 'the books he wrote', but can also mean 'the books he published' or 'the books he designed', or 'the books he printed' (though *books by John* will be interpreted as 'books he wrote' rather than as 'books he printed'). If the relation expressed shifts still further to 'some inherent relation' — of which actual 'possession' is only one — or 'some non-inherent relation' the interpretational possibilities become accordingly more dependent on features of the lexical elements involved, or on the imagination: *John's books* in (28) might refer to books he possesses, but alternatively also to books he is studying from, or the books he brought with him when he entered the room. Finally, in a sentence like

(32) He missed his train and arrived late

the relation expressed by *his train* does not seem to indicate more than some vague relation of 'appurtenance' (Schwartz 1968:752) and furthermore, does not paraphrase very well. Any paraphrase is here more awkward and less precise than the expression itself. This would argue in favor of the viewpoint that this kind of ambiguity-by-vagueness is better explained by the assump-

---

[11] As it is correctly observed by Kuryłowicz in his discussion of the genitive (1964: 187): 'The loss of purely *syntactic* motivation entails the increase of the role of *semantic* context, i.e. of the meaning of the two nouns' (author's italics).

tion that the relation expressed by the adnominal possessive *is* vague, than by assuming that it is inherently ambiguous.

4.1.2. *Ambiguity and linguistic specification*

It is understandable that problems of the kind discussed here have arisen especially in the context of Transformational grammar, and that transformationalists seem ready to regard any residual ambiguity as a hidden defect of the description rather than to consider that in some cases ambiguities could be explained as inherent vagueness. After all, many of these problems are inherent in the very notion of derivation which is a cornerstone of the theory.

Another reason, however, is the requirement that a linguistic description should provide each sentence, in the sense of 'string of elements', with its unique structural description[12]. If this is taken in the sense that the linguistic description ought to explain all the interpretations a native speaker might give to a particular sentence, it entails a major problem. There can, in my opinion, be little doubt that there are interpretations of a sentence or of one particular grammatical relation, that are explainable only by leaving some things unspecified — and here I still leave out of consideration exact referential specifications in language use. Formulated otherwise, the requirement that the deep structure determines the interpretation of a sentence, and that more than one interpretation should therefore correspond with more than one deep structure, becomes ambiguous in itself as soon as less clear-cut cases of ambiguity than grammatical homonymy are involved. It can be interpreted as a requirement that the interpretations of a sentence are *specified* unambiguously as so many inherent meanings, or, alternatively, as a requirement that the inherent meaning of a sentence is described in such a fashion that the various interpretations it could have *follow from* its description, even when there is no one-to-one correspondence between the possible interpretations of the sentence and the distinctions made in that description. These two requirements, it should be emphasized, are not at all the same, either in practice or in theory[13].

What is at stake here is not only the question of whether in the description of a particular sentence we assume one, two, or three inherent distinctions,

---

[12] The preoccupation with ambiguity may originally have been motivated by certain mathematical properties of context-free phrase structure grammars. See Chomsky (1963: 387 ff.) and Greibach (1963).

[13] Within the framework of Transformational grammar also, opinions diverge quite fundamentally. Compare Chomsky's defence of the 'lexicalist' position against the 'transformationalist' position in the description of nominalizations, in Chomsky (1970); compare also Newmeyer's discussion of *begin* and related verbs in Newmeyer (1969).

but also the more general question of how the various interpretations of a sentence can be accounted for without over-specifying its meaning. For those linguists for whom the sentence is not by definition the upper bound of a linguistic description, the problem is accordingly less acute. Whether they have solved it is another matter; but it is clear that a description of the ambiguities of a sentence like *He saw the girl with the white hat* along the lines sketched above, avoids some rather awkward problems of over-specification[14].

4.2. Neutralization

In itself, of course, the problem of whether a grammatical construction represents one or more than one grammatical relation is not new, It has been discussed extensively under the term 'neutralization', especially in the context of the description of 'overt' grammatical categories, such as the case-endings of inflecting languages.

The term 'neutralization' in grammatical analysis was formed in analogy with Trubetzkoy's 'Aufhebung der phonologische Oppositionen'[15]. This very starting point is, I believe, one of the reasons why this discussion has never been satisfactory since undue emphasis was laid on morphological identity and on isolated paradigms.

When neutralization in the area of grammatical analysis has been viewed as a phenomenon parallel to 'neutralization' in phonology, its definition has often taken the following form. When in some language a systematic difference in 'function' corresponds with a systematically attestable difference in 'form', and when in one subpart of the paradigm the systematic difference in form is not attested, the corresponding difference in function is also 'neutralized'. The classic example in this connection is the neutralization of the Nominative/ Accusative distinction in Latin Nouns in the neuter paradigm.

This definition takes the correlation of form and function as a starting point, but still leaves room for considerable variation in the ways in which the criterion is put to use in actual description. The special issue of the Travaux de l'Institut de Linguistique de Paris devoted to the neutralization problem (Martinet 1957) offers an almost bewildering variety of opinions on for instance such examples as French *il mange/ils mangent*[16]. In principle, the

---

[14] Also Bach's assumption that noun phrases are relative clauses in the deep structure, seems to be largely motivated by the ambiguity problem. As far as his two Tense elements are concerned, his analysis is bound to run into serious difficulties just with simple sentences like *He saw the president*. Whether this refers to 'the THEN president' or to 'the NOW president' depends on extra-linguistic data only in many contexts.

[15] See Trubetzkoy (1939:69 ff. and 206 ff.).

[16] For a recent discussion see Mok (1968a).

analogy with phonological neutralization can lead to rather extreme positions.

According to one view, it is maintained that whenever an 'overt' difference in form is 'absent', the grammatical distinction originally correlated with the formal distinction is also 'neutralized'. This view has, at least theoretically, been defended by Hjelmslev (1939;1961) and by Cantineau[17]. It has been attacked in an article by Godel (1948) and in various articles by Bazell[18]. Their main objections – which, in my opinion, are completely justified – can be summarized as follows: There is no reason to assume that there is a state of symmetry between form and function in any natural language; in the case of neutralization, that from the absence of a formal opposition one can conclude the absence of a functional distinction. This methodological and theoretical objection has been stressed in particular by Bazell, who has labelled the view under attack a 'correspondence fallacy' (see Bazell 1952). Grammatical analysis, or, in general, the analysis of 'meaningful' oppositions should decide from criteria derived from its own level whether or not some grammatical construction represents 'one' or 'more than one' grammatical relation.

As soon as the strict analogy between phonological and grammatical neutralization is abandoned, there will be cases where the natural conclusion to be drawn is that some grammatical constructions, though 'same' in terms of morphology or constituent structure, are 'non-same', or, homonymous grammatically. It is, for instance, not self-evident why the distinction between Nominative and Accusative in Latin should lose its syntactic relevance in the Neuter paradigm. This does not necessarily mean that 'homonymies' are always completely 'accidental'. It may be defended, for instance[19] that the absence of the distinction Nominative/Accusative in neuter nouns in Latin and other Indo-European languages is governed by a deeper distinction 'Ergative' vs. 'Non-Ergative' which in general is relevant only for nouns that have a feature (+Animate), and that the Nominative in the non-neuter paradigms, is in fact a reflection of the category 'Ergative'. This illustrates that the application of grammatical rather than phonological criteria does not necessarily settle the issue unequivocally; in this case, it would depend on one's view concerning which grammatical distinction takes precedence over the other. But without criteria that derive from the description of sentences themselves and from the grammatical pattern of the language, the issue cannot even be profitably approached.

[17] See for instance his article 'Les oppositions significatives' (1952).

[18] Bazell (1949a;1949b;1952;1954:337 ff.).

[19] The arguments are summarized in Martinet (1962:149 ff.). See also Anderson (1968a:27).

Another consequence of the phonological approach to the neutralization problem in grammatical description is, that with many authors it is unclear what 'neutralization' exactly means.

Hjelmslev, for instance, states that the neutralization of the Nominative/ Accusative distinction in e.g. Lat. *templum* is the analogous manifestation of the neutralization of the distinction Voiced/Voiceless in word-final consonants in Danish and other Germanic languages. He adds that the grammatical syncretism is 'resolvable' by analogical inference (1961:91), that is, on comparing *templum* in its different occurrences with, say, *domus* and *domum*. His highly abstract terminology, however, obscures the answer to the crucial question: whether or not *templum* is to be viewed as syntactically homonymous. From his statement that a chain of elements where the resolvable syncretisms would indeed be resolved is the 'idealized' chain, but that the chain of elements where the syncretisms remain unresolved is the 'actualized' chain, no definite conclusion about this question can be inferred. The same, in my opinion, is true for his formulation (ibid., p. 90) 'the syncretism of nominative and accusative has the meaning 'nominative-accusative'[20]. There is a fundamental ambiguity here, by which for some authors 'neutralization' is simply a synonym for homonymy, whereas with other authors it apparently means a functionally motivated absence of a certain grammatical distinction[21]. For the purposes of a grammatical description, these two phenomena are not at all equivalent.

This brings us to the second problem inherent in the use of the term neutralization. When the condition that functional differences should of necessity correlate with formally attestable distinctions at all points, is dropped, but the analogy with phonological neutralization persists, this may lead — and has led, I would say — to the application of a criterion of 'internal symmetry of grammatical pattern'. And that has equally undesirable consequences.

This view is held by Bloomfield and can best be formulated by quoting him: 'The existence of even a single overdifferentiated paradigm implies homonymy in the regular paradigms' (1935:224). As pointed out already by Nida in 1948[22] and also in an article by Bazell (1949b:225), this principle is in the

[20] A similar formulation is to be found in Hjelmslev (1939:54-55).

[21] In his article on neutralizations in the verbal system of Greek, Ruipérez (1953) convincingly argues that a distinction should be made between 'coincidental' homonymy and functionally motivated neutralization.

[22] For another formulation of the moderate view, see Robins (1970:59). As Nida observes, the position somewhere in between the extremes has the undeniable disadvantage that it can hardly be defined. His conclusion that in practice it is nevertheless unavoidable to me seems to be correct.

last resort equally as untenable as the foregoing. It would, in a strict sense,
imply that the English pronouns *I* and *you* are homonymous with respect to
the distinction Male/Female which is formally present in the third person
pronouns *he* vs. *she*. It is obvious that *I* can refer either to a speaker who is
Male or to a speaker who is Female. There is, however, no point in describ-
ing the pronouns *I* and *you* as homonyms, even if, in some particular context,
the use of *I* or of *you* might lead to an actual interpretational ambiguity. A
more natural solution for such cases is to assume that the distinction Male/
Female, formally attestable in the third person pronouns of the Singular, is an
opposition which is 'isolated', in the Trubetzkoyan terminology, and has no
consequences for the description of *I* and *you*. Furthermore, the distribution
of the Male/Female distinction in the pronoun system of English corresponds
with a universal tendency (see Greenberg 1966a[2]:96) for this distinction to
be more often overtly expressed in pronouns referring to 'the person who is
neither the Speaker or the Adressee' than for persons referring to either the
Speaker or the Adressee. It is tempting – but of course speculative – to regard
this as a case of neutralization, in the sense of absence of a distinction, that
might have a semi-natural explanation, since for a pronoun referring to the
'Speaker' in direct discourse the distinction feels more redundant.

The example given here is admittedly extreme, and I do not wish to imply
that Bloomfield would in practice have defended the view that *I* is a homonym. But it is difficult to see how such conclusions can, in principle, be
avoided if his criterion quoted above, were to apply throughout. Therefore,
the example can serve to illustrate that the criterion of 'internal symmetry'
cannot apply without at the same time added restrictions that, just like the
criterion itself, derive from the description of the grammatical system under
consideration[23].

The problem inherent in Bloomfield's formulation is not restricted to the
'paradigmatic' approach to grammatical categories. It is still a quite wide-
spread tendency to assume that grammatical systems of natural languages are
symmetrical in the sense that a distinction in one place must have a correlate
somewhere else[24], and that an element that can be interpreted in more than
one way is therefore homonymous. The fundamental objection against this

---

[23] Notice that Hjelmslev's criterion of analogical inference will in practice yield the
very same result.
[24] Kraak's assumption (1966:89) that there is a one-to-one correspondence between
positive and negative sentences leads to unnecessary complications in the syntactic
analysis of positive sentences. See Bazell (1949a:144, fn. 1), for some comments on the
dangers inherent in the 'symmetrical' view of grammatical systems.

view is that it does not allow for a distinction between accidental neutralization, functionally motivated neutralization, and neutrality in the sense of lack of specification or mere vagueness.

4.2.1. *Nouns and pronouns*

Even the most recent literature testifies that these difficulties are not imaginatory. A problem which in fact is closely related to the one mentioned above arises when the Male/Female distinction of third person pronouns, whether demonstrative or possessive, is transferred to Nouns and Noun Phrases. The motivation for this can be twofold: (i) in many contexts, nouns and noun phrases with third person pronouns share the feature that they refer to 'somebody who is neither the Speaker nor the Addressee', (ii) there are nouns, like *messenger-boy* on the one hand and *stewardess* on the other hand, that are self-classificatory as far as the distinction Male/Female is concerned. Consequently, there seems no harm in the assumption that Male/Female is a 'covert' opposition in English nouns, or, that all nouns where the distinction is not overtly expressed, are still inherently ambiguous in this respect. They can accordingly be specified in the lexicon as (+Male v −Male), where 'v' is the disjunctive 'or'.

It has been brought to attention by McCawley (1968:136 ff.) that there are at least two reasons why this is inadequate. As is well known this device was originally introduced in Transformational grammar to ensure the automatic and correct generation of sentences like

(33a) My neighbour hurt himself
(33b) My neighbour hurt herself

or

(34a) My neighbour lost his bicycle
(34b) My neighbour lost her bicycle

In that framework of Transformational description where it is assumed that the reflexive pronoun in such sentences actually 'replaces' a Noun Phrase in the underlying structure that is identical to the Subject Noun Phrase, there is no other solution than to assume that all Nouns have a specification in the deep structure (+Male v −Male), since otherwise there is no motivation for the choice of *his* or *her, himself* or *herself*.

Against this, McCawley has argued essentially: (i) that the choice of the correct pronoun in these cases is not a matter of a specification in the deep structure of the sentence[25] but that it is determined by non-linguistic factors

[25] For footnote, see next page.

of reference, (ii) that the solution is inadequate anyway. It would entail that the same nouns, *neighbour, teacher, doctor,* etc. are also inherently ambiguous in sentences like

(35a) My neighbour is fat
(35b) My doctor lives next door

Once the nouns in question are listed in the lexicon as (+Male v −Male), it is unavoidable that the sentences (35a) and (35b) are also inherently ambiguous in this respect. But this consequence is unacceptable since sentences like (35a) and (35b) do not appear ambiguous at all for native speakers.

I will not go into the exact nature of the alternative solutions proposed by McCawley, the more so since the objectives of his paper are not the objectives of this book. His standpoint, however, that the correct choice of pronouns in sentences like the one quoted above is determined by context rather than by semantic or grammatical specifications in the deep structure, seems to be perfectly in accordance with the deictic and anaphoric nature of these elements[26].

The dilemma pointed out in McCawley's paper illustrates once more that a device which can account for an ambiguity in some places, more often than not has the disadvantage of being too powerful in other places. A theoretically not unimportant consequence of his position with regard to the functioning of pronouns is, that the requirement one comes across quite often in Transformational literature that the deep structure of a sentence should be unambiguous semantically[27], can only be understood in a relative sense, and is otherwise difficult to maintain.

Furthermore, sentences like (35a) and (35b) quoted above, are only two of presumably many cases where ambiguity is not just a matter of 'inherent polysemy'. It can safely be assumed that a speaker of English can be made aware of the fact that the pronoun *you* or the noun phrases *our teacher* can refer to somebody who is Male or to somebody who is Female. But it is quite another thing to conclude that these elements should therefore be regarded as

[25] A similar conclusion with regard to the status of pronouns in the deep structure was reached in Jackendoff (1968).

[26] Many of the problems connected with the use of referential indices in the deep structure to indicate anaphoric relations might have been avoided if it had been recognized from the start that the assumption that pronouns are 'replacives' is basically wrong, though its credentials are old. See Dik (1968b:79) for some pertinent remarks on this point.

[27] Cf. for instance Weinreich (1966b:399): 'Semantic theories can and should be so formulated as to guarantee that deep structures (including their lexical components) are specified as unambiguous in the first place'.

inherently ambiguous in the linguistic description. Some caution is in order, not only with regard to the transference of oppositions from one category to another category, but also with regard to the readiness with which it is sometimes taken for granted that a distinction which can be assumed to be 'relevant' for a native speaker should therefore have its reflection in the description of the grammatical categories of his language. Of course, it is not easy to evaluate to what extent a sentence like

(35b) My doctor lives next door

is ambiguous for native speakers in the same way as the sentence

(3) He hit the man with the stick

is. But even if it were the case that the one ambiguity is on occasion just as relevant as the other — though I am inclined to doubt that this would be the case —, it is still a perfectly reasonable requirement to impose on a linguistic description that it makes a *distinction* between the one ambiguity and the other ambiguity.

4.2.2. *Kinds of ambiguity*

The problem posed can be illustrated with many other examples. I will assume, however, that the point I am driving at has become somewhat clearer by now. Sentences of a natural language offer many ambiguities, but these ambiguities are not all equivalent in terms of the linguistic description. Since they are not, this should be recognized.

In grammatical analysis, an ambiguity can be called structural in the sense that a sentence can be regarded as 'homonymous' whenever it represents more than one grammatical relation. This is the case in the example

(3) He hit the man with the stick

which is homonymous between an Adverbial and an Adjectival interpretation of *with the stick*, and in the example

(36) The shooting of the hunters was terrible

which is homonymous between a Subjective and an Objective interpretation. But even these two structural ambiguities are not mutually equivalent. The homonymy of the first sentence can be resolved without residue; apart from a possible 'deep' relation between *with*-phrases in general, then, such an homonymy may be referred to as fortuitous. Homonymies of the type *the shooting of the hunters* are not resolvable without residue, since *of the hunters* is a Modifier to *the shooting* under either interpretation. This is even more conspicuous in the constructions with the adnominal possessive, like

(30) John's assassination

Furthermore, as we saw above (p. 100), the relationship, which in some cases can indeed be labelled grammatically 'Subjective', in other cases, like

(37) John's books

can shift from the interpretation 'written by' to the interpretation 'manufactured by', whereas in examples like

(38) John's cries

it means no more than something like 'proceeding from': in those cases the use of the term 'Subjective' becomes problematic since the relationship with a clear-cut grammatical opposition suggested by the term, has become rather tenuous[28].

Secondly, the one and the same grammatical relation can still be semantically ambiguous. Let us call such ambiguities systematic as long as the interpretational differences correlate with one or more *semantic* subcategories involved in the same *grammatical* relation. Thus, the relation expressed in the noun phrase

(39) the girl with the flowers

can indicate some 'inherent' relation or some 'accidental' relation: the girl can be regularly associated with the selling of flowers, or she may just have bought some flowers. A reason for calling this ambiguity systematic is that the distinction can also be found with other constructions like the adnominal possessive. Compare e.g.

(40) the bull with the long horns / its horns
(41) the man with the martini / his martini

More often than not, the interpretation will be determined by the nature of the lexical elements involved, but the distinction between inherent and non-inherent 'have' will also lead to ambiguities. The phrase

[28] Though the tendency to see analogies is quite persistent. Anderson (1968b:312) proposes to derive *my mother* from a structure underlying *the woman who bore me*, which strikes me as implausible. The first question is whether 'woman who bore me' *is* an adequate characterization of the meaning of *my mother*. But even if it were, regarding the relation as syntactic is not without its problems. It would imply that the deep structure underlying *my mother* is radically different from the one underlying *my child*, and, as far as I can see, that the verbs in the underlying structures of *my mother* and *my father* are non-identical as well. Both implications are counter-intuitive.

(42) the man with the camera

is quite naturally ambiguous between the relatively systematic interpretations 'the man who carries some camera' and 'the camera-man'. The phrase

(43) the man with the wooden leg

is more unexpectedly ambiguous between the interpretations 'the man who has a wooden leg' and 'the man who carries a wooden leg around'.

Thirdly, let us call an ambiguity unsystematic or indeterminate in those cases where a grammatical relation only indicates a possible range of interpretations, without any more precise specification. The phrase

(39) the girl with the flowers

can still be interpreted as 'the girl that is decorated with flowers', or 'the girl that is trying to sell flowers', or 'the girl that carries flowers in her hand', or 'the girl that is strewing flowers on the street', etc. In these cases, the relation between the grammatical category and the possible interpretations is a one-many relationship which cannot be specified except at the cost of a loss of adequacy.

Finally, let us call an ambiguity merely referential in those cases where the interpretation intended is solely derivable from non-linguistic data. If *the girl with the flowers* refers to 'some contextually definite girl with flowers', it is undecidable on the basis of that sentence alone which girl it is, and in those cases where there might be more than one, the sentence can be ambiguous. A suitable illustration of the latter kind of ambiguity is the famous pronouncement of the Delphi oracle

(44) Croesus by crossing the Halys will ruin a mighty realm

which led to considerable confusion and even to the downfall of an empire, though grammatically the sentence is perfectly unambiguous (Aristotle, *Ars rhetorica* 1407a).

A corollary to this distinction between 'kinds' of ambiguity is that neutralization in grammatical analysis should mean quite different things.

In the case of sentence (3), a difference in syntactic structure is neutralized by word order only. This would be an instance of neutralization in the sense of an accidental absence of the formal correlate of a functional distinction.

In the case of sentence (36), the distinction between Subjective and Objective is neutralized by the optional absence of an Agent in the Objective interpretation. This is slightly different from an accidental neutralization by mere restrictions on word order. The optional absence of an Agent is a characteristic of Passive sentences as well. Therefore, one might entertain the possibility that structures like *the shooting of the hunters* are not just fortuitously homonymous, but that their neutrality is connected with a deeper-seated grammatical feature of the language under consideration[29].

In those cases where one and the same relation, say an inherent relation expressed in the phrase *with the N* allows for different interpretations, the term neutralization is suitable only if one understands by it that the absence of certain distinctions is a feature inherent in that grammatical structure. It is not accidental that nominalizations lack grammatical specifications to be found in verbal constructions, such as Tense features, or that they do not specify semantically what can be so specified with Verbs.

4.3. Grammar, ambiguity, and the lexicon

Thus far, I have more or less tacitly assumed what may be referred to as Hockett's condition (III): when a sentence is regarded as grammatically homonymous, the difference in interpretation is not to be relegated to a difference in meaning between its lexical elements. In Hockett's terms: we will regard 'hierarchical structure' as a primitive of the description because it explains ambiguities which cannot be explained lexically, and because, in general, it explains grammatical structure without reliance upon such cumbersome notions as meaning, probability, context, and speaker's intentions.

This condition too deserves some further consideration. Since Hockett wrote this, other linguists have stressed the 'autonomy' of grammatical structure vis-à-vis the lexicon even further. There is reason to believe that they are right but there is also reason to believe that they are right only if 'autonomy' is understood in a modified sense.

The fact that it is profitable, and unavoidable, for reasons of generalization, to assign more than one grammatical structure to one and the same linguistic expression, does not entail, on the other hand, that lexical elements do not also eventually play a rôle in many cases of grammatical homonymy.

To take up Hockett's example once more, it is unquestionable that the ambiguity of

(45) old men and women

is somewhat more plausible than the ambiguity of

(46) old men and babies

---

[29] See e.g. Lyons (1968:371).

since

(46a) old babies and old men

is somewhat odd. In contradistinction to cases where ambiguities are ruled out because categorial features of lexical elements are involved, we would, in a case like (46) rather say that what is involved here is a somewhat more idiosyncratic feature, let us say (Young) of *baby* or just a presupposition, which makes the ambiguity less probable. Cf. also the possible ambiguities of

(47) John loves old cities and villages
(48) ?John loves old cities and landscapes
(49) ?John loves old port and coca cola

Here, then, the problem arises concerning the extent to which 'grammatical homonymy' is matched by 'ambiguity' in actual interpretation, and vice versa. Consider the following sentences:

(50) He hit the man with the stick
(51) He hit the man with the scar
(52) He hit the man with the beard

At first sight, it is reasonable to say that (50) is ambiguous between the Adnominal and Adverbial interpretation of *with the stick*, whereas (51) is not; *with the scar* can only be attributive to *the man*, and not Instrumental. On a second examination, there appears to be a problem that is entailed by (52). It is, after all, not inconceivable that somebody hits somebody in the face with a false beard. If, however, it is agreed that (52) cóuld have both interpretations, this changes the picture somewhat in the other two sentences. From an interpretational point of view, we are now inclined to say not that (50) *is* ambiguous, and that (51) is *not* ambiguous, but that (50) most probably is ambiguous, that (51) most probably is not ambiguous, and that (52) is a borderline case.

   This, of course, is a very brief restatement of a very familiar problem, which is entailed by the assumption that grammatical structure is a 'primitive' and therefore relatively autonomous. Do we exclude the 'Instrumental' interpretation of (51), for instance by putting a restriction on *scar* in its description in the lexicon to prevent it from ever being able to be Instrumental after verbs like *hit*, or do we allow *scar* to be used after *hit* just like *stick* or *fist*, as far as grammatical structure is concerned?

   The first solution, which on various occasions has been proposed (Katz and Fodor 1964; Chomsky 1965) is feasible, but onerous. It is true that, in a description that is generative in the sense that it generates all sentences of the language and does not generate all its non-sentences, some lexical elements cannot be allowed to co-occur in particular grammatical frameworks. In practice, however, the strict view on this requirement leads to horrible complexities. In this case, for instance, it would amount to indexing all Inanimate Objects and body parts with which you do not normally hit somebody. The price to be paid is higher than the advantage gained, which is one perfectly legitimate reason to doubt the validity of the principle.

There is, however, also a theoretically more significant reason for dropping this condition. The Instrumental interpretation of

(51) He hit the man with the scar

may be highly improbable, far-fetched, odd, bizarre, difficult to conceive of, but it is not impossible. On the contrary, the very fact that we can consider two possibilities, and reject one of them, tells us something about the relative autonomy of grammatical structure. It is always possible that somebody might say

(53) He hit me with Sheila

meaning that 'he' threw poor Sheila at me, or might say

(54) He looked at the girl with the stick

and adds 'but he didn't see much', implying that somebody was fruitless trying to use a wooden stick as a telescope. Whether or not such garden party jokes (Hockett 1961:226) are funny should be of little concern to linguists. The Instrumental interpretation of (54) is not very probable, but that is not the same as impossible. Many puns, descriptions of bizarre situations, good poetry, and the techniques of not a few entertainers rest upon the possibility of making unusual use of usual means[30].

Recognizing this does not entail that grammatical structure is autonomous in the sence of 'independent'. To neutralize the power of structure-assigning rules, various constraints will have to be imposed on them. The ambiguity of

(3) He hit the man with the stick

---

[30] Numerous instances of the kind of word-play I have in mind are to be found in the works of Lewis Carroll. Compare the following passage from *Sylvie and Bruno* (quoted in Sutherland 1970:168):
'It singed right *froo*. I *sawed* it singing with its long beard...'.
  'It couldn't sing with its *beard*', I said, hoping to puzzle the little fellow, ' a beard isn't a *voice*'. 'Well then, *oo* couldn't walk with Sylvie', Bruno cried triumphantly, 'Sylvie isn't a *foot*!'

between an Instrumental and an Adjectival interpretation of the *with*-phrase, for instance, requires, at least in the Singular, that the two determiners of the head noun and its modifying noun phrase are identical[31]. The sentence

(3a) He hit the man with a stick

has only the Instrumental interpretation. But the impossibility of interpreting the *with*-phrase in (3a) as Adjectival is on a different level from the 'impossibility' of interpreting the *with*-phrase in (51) as Instrumental.

I would therefore agree with the standpoint expressed in McCawley (1968a, passim) that many of the originally proposed selectional restrictions are too idiosyncratic or have too much to do with extra linguistic data rather than with linguistic features, to be built into the linguistic description as restrictions on its generative capacity[32]. I would equally agree with the view defended in Weinreich (1966b:416) that a linguistic description should, on the contrary, be allowed to generate sentences that will receive strange, unusual, and hard to conceive of interpretations. This includes, as Weinreich observes, those sentences that can only be understood 'metaphorically', in the sense that the co-occurrence of two lexical elements within one grammatical framework, forces a non-literal interpretation upon the native speaker. Selectional restrictions should be allowed to exclude grammatical relationship only as long as they do not exclude sentences or interpretations of sentences that are perfectly interpretable.

In the context of Transformational grammar, this problem was, as far as I know, first stated clearly by Ziff[33]. To quote his example once more, a linguistic description that has to decide whether or not the sentence

(55) The shooting of the elephants was terrible

is ambiguous, and decides that it is not, since elephants cannot be imagined as handling guns, is guilty of over-specification.

A similar problem arises with Fillmore's statement (Fillmore 1968:24,

---

[31] Another constraint is that the possibility of interpreting the Adjectival *with*-phrases as 'Appositive', in sentences like *He saw the man with the stick,* disappears in sentences with a (+Affective) or (-Stative) verb like *hit*.

[32] Hockett's statement (1961:221) that 'any fact about a sentence used by a hearer in parsing a sentence is a grammatical fact' is certainly too strong.

[33] Harman (1966) discusses some of Ziff's arguments and conclusions, but evades the basic issue. The question of the interrelations between grammatical structure, lexical meaning, and extra linguistic data is discussed in a most fundamental manner in Reichling's paper on 'essential' and 'accidental' rules of grammar; see Reichling (1939).

fn. 32) that the Noun in Instrumental *with*-phrases is typically (−Animate). He himself adduces counterexamples like

(56) I rapped him on the head with a snake

He adds as a comment that such sentences can only be interpreted under the assumption that the deep structure is something like 'with the body of...', which suggests that cases where the Noun is (+Animate) are somewhat deviant. This, I would say, depends on the way you look at it. The other way to look at it would be this, that the grammatical category Instrumental is sufficiently autonomous to allow some Animate Nouns also in Instrumental *with*-phrases. Sentences like

(57) Caesar put the Helvetians to flight with fifty soldiers

do not seem deviant at all.

This finally, tells us something about the linguistic description of ambiguity in general. We started from the assumption that a linguistic description should be capable of assigning more than one grammatical structure to one and the same sentence. For reasons of generative description and generalization, this is an important requirement. But it turns out − as might have been suspected from the beginning − that on examining each individual sentence, it is not as straightforward a procedure as we might wish. Some lexical elements can, for grammatical purposes, be categorically distinguished so that sentences can be excluded as not well-forced, or, in other cases, one interpretation of a sentence can be exluded. But as soon as probability, idiosyncratic features of meaning, or even knowledge of 'things' referred to by lexical elements rather than their inherent sense, are concerned, there is a problem. The most a linguistic description can achieve in such cases, is, to indicate the conditions under which a sentence is *potentially* ambiguous inasfar as its grammatical structure is involved. The actual decision as to whether such a sentence *does* or *does not* have two meanings for native speakers, depends on factors that are outside the domain of a description of sentences in isolation.

5. AMBIGUITY AND THE LEXICON: SOME OBSERVATIONS ON POLYSEMY

5.1. Preliminary remarks

An important source of ambiguity in natural language is the polysemy of lexical elements, and this is certainly one of the most intricate problems of semantic description. It is easy to observe that many words[1] in many sentences can be understood quite differently, but it is notoriously difficult to give a systematic account of this phenomenon in a description of a language. I will restrict myself in this chapter to some preliminary observations on the polysemy problem, in connection with the description of ambiguity.

Let me point out at the beginning that 'polysemous' and 'ambiguous' will not be regarded here as equivalent notions. In the field of lexical description also, terms like 'polysemous', 'ambiguous', and 'having more than one interpretation' are often used as if they were interchangeable. Thereby they become cover terms that indicate linguistically quite different kinds of ambiguity. I have argued in the foregoing chapters, in connection with certain problems of grammatical analysis, that it is the task of a linguistic description to make the differences between kinds of ambiguity more explicit; I will act upon the same assumption in this chapter.

To achieve this goal, I believe it is necessary first of all to maintain a basic distinction between the content of a sentence and its interpretation. By the content of a sentence[2] I will understand: the inherent semantic structure of a sentence as a type, such as it is specified in a linguistic description. By the interpretation of a sentence I will understand the various ways in which one and the same sentence can be understood in each unique case of language use. It is

---

[1] 'Word' is used in this chapter not in its grammatical sense, but for 'basic semantic unit of the lexicon', or, for *lexeme* as it is defined by Lyons (1968:197 ff.). Under this definition, *book* and *books* will be regarded as two different forms of the same lexeme BOOK.

[2] I follow Reichling here in his distinction between 'betekenis' of lexical elements, 'inhoud' of phrases and sentences, and 'interpretatie' in language use. Many of the ideas on polysemy put forward here originate from Reichling's discussions of semantic description as they are to be found in Reichling (1935, 1969[5], esp. pp. 25-33 and 52-60), and various unpublished University lectures.

unfortunate, I think, that the well-established term 'interpretation' is nowa-
days often used for what I refer to here as the inherent 'content' of a sentence.

As a corollary to this distinction, I will distinguish between (i) the inherent
meaning of a lexical element — its full specification in the lexicon —, (ii) the
possible further specification of its inherent meaning in the context of a particular sentence, (iii) the possible further specification in the interpretation of a
sentence in language use. Some lexical elements that can be understood in
more than one way will accordingly be represented in the lexicon with distinct
entries corresponding to their various senses. But the mere fact *that* a lexical
element can, on different occasions, be understood in more than one way, is
not in itself a sufficient reason to represent it as having more than one distinct
'sense'. To cut the question short, I will henceforth use the term 'inherently
polysemous' only to refer to lexical elements for which more than one entry is
given in the lexicon.

I think that these first distinctions may help to clarify the ambiguity issue
somewhat, but far be it from me to suggest that the ambiguity problem can be
solved by mere terminological readjustment. The distinction between 'inherent
polysemy' and other forms of ambiguity is more of a guiding principle than a
concept that can be used a priori, and the boundary is difficult to establish.
The verb *hate* will be understood differently in the sentences *I hate soup, I
hate Kathy*, and *I hate lies*, but we may wonder whether this entails *hate*
having different senses or whether these different interpretations are only contextual specializations of one and the same sense. The word *old* is understood
differently in *an old man* ('of a relatively great age'), *an old shoe* ('not new'),
and *an old custom* ('dating from early times'); it is quite reasonable to conclude that *old* has distinct senses, though of course these senses are related.
The word *big*[3] can mean, roughly paraphrased, 'large' or it can mean 'momen-
tous, important', and here the relation between the senses is much less gradual,
though still not nonexistent.

Weinreich (1966b:411-2) writes that it is doubtful whether 'an absolute
distinction between true ambiguity and mere indefiniteness of reference' can
be maintained as a primitive concept in semantic theory; I feel that it is nevertheless imperative that a semantic description should strive towards such a
distinction.

The first task to undertake here is the distinction between polysemy on the
one hand and vagueness and generality on the other hand.

---

[3] For an analysis of the different senses of *big*, and a discussion of inherent polysemy
and contextual specification, see Lamb 1964.

5.1.1. *Vagueness*

Following a suggestion of Chao's (1959:1)[4], let us assume that the meaning of a lexical element is vague inasmuch as its range of referential application is not unambiguously delimited. To quote one of Chao's examples, native speakers can argue over the question of whether the colour of a particular dress is yellow or brown. Colour terms more or less arbitrarily encode the division of a continuum[5], and the very fact of such division will entail borderline cases. In those cases where vagueness is undesirable, other terms can be added to the repertoire to refer to intermediate shades of colours, or to nuances of the same colour. Such terms allow for greater preciseness, but they also magnify the problem of vagueness, since the addition of distinctions multiplies the borderline cases.

Vagueness, or 'overlapping of domains' as it is described by Black, is a quite common phenomenon. Within certain semantic fields – as for instance the field of kinship terms – the referential range of a word may be unambiguously limited by convention, and in other cases the range of application of a vague word may be determined ad hoc. Apart from this, vagueness is the rule rather than the exception. It can be disputed whether or not an unusually large volume of a scientific journal is to be called a book, and what the criteria are upon which to decide whether a story is to be called a novel or a novelette, not to speak of the traditional controversies over the meaning of words like *knowledge* or *freedom*. Such disputes are not the linguist's concern: the conclusion to be drawn is not that the words involved are inherently polysemous, but that inherent in their meaning there is a certain vagueness of referential applicability.

5.1.2. *Generality*

A second feature of lexical elements that may give rise to ambiguity in actual use without entailing these words having different senses is generality. Quoting once more from Chao, the word *coloured* can be ambiguous in language use since it does not indicate which colour or colours are meant; the sentence *I brought an animal from the Zoo* can be ambiguous in language use since it may arouse curiosity which animal the speaker brought. Between lexical elements like *animal* and *monkey*, or *coloured* and *yellow*, a paradigmatic relationship of hyponymy or sense-inclusion can be defined (see Lyons 1968:453 ff.). In language use, subordinate terms like *yellow* and *monkey*

---

[4] Cf. also Black (1949).

[5] Actually, the status of colour terms is somewhat more complicated, but this does not affect the example given.

may resolve a lack of clarity since they can specify what is left unspecified by the use of the superordinate term: *a yellow dress* is more specific than *a coloured dress*, and *I brought a monkey from the Zoo* is more specific than *I brought an animal from the Zoo*. It would, however, be an error to conclude that words like *coloured* and *animal* are therefore inherently polysemous. *Coloured* does not mean '(blue ∨ red ∨ green ∨ ...)', nor does it mean '(blue ∧ red ∧ green ∧ ...)'. It means, roughly paraphrased, and disregarding its non-literal senses, 'with colours' or 'not without colours' (or perhaps, as Lyons observes (o.c., p. 456) it is in some cases just an antonym of *white*). If one considers such words as *coloured, animal, tree,* one realizes that it could lead to descriptive absurdities to maintain that they ambiguously represent the meanings of the more specific terms to which they are related, and that a sentence like *He carried five trees to the garden* is therefore inherently ambiguous[6]. Since it cannot be denied that hyponymy is an important structural principle in a description of sense relations between elements in the lexicon, it would follow that one cannot define the inherent *meaning* of an element in terms of its sense *relations* with other elements alone.

However, the distinction between generality and ambiguity is not so easy to make in every case. To maintain that *child* is ambiguous for native speakers as between 'daughter' and 'son' or that *friend* is ambiguous between 'Male friend' and 'Female friend', is less absurd than to maintain that *tree* is ambiguous because it does not specify which kind of tree. In the case of *friend*, the possibilities are, firstly, exhausted by the one opposition Male/Female, and secondly, this opposition is a reflection of a structural principle realized in other places in the language system. I have argued above (ch. 4, p. 106), that it would be wrong to regard words like *friend* as inherently polysemous inasfar as the dinstinction Male/Female is concerned; like other general terms, they may very well be used in contexts where a certain difference is felt to be irrelevant (Chao 1959:1). But it cannot be denied that, in language use, implicational relationships between superordinate and subordinate terms can make themselves felt more in some cases than in others[7].

---

[6] Nor does, of course, the meaning of a general term change under its different applications. Such conclusion rests upon a confusion of meaning and reference, as was conclusively pointed out by Reichling (1935:247-51) in a critique of Stern (1931:35 ff.). For another discussion of polysemy vs. generality, see Bolinger (1961b:13-22).

[7] Another example of what might be called an ambiguity by supposition is presented by the Dutch kinship term *oom*, 'uncle'. This refers either to 'brother of one of the parents' or to 'husband of a parent's sister', and hence is ambiguous as between 'blood relative' and 'other kind of relative'. The very useful notion 'ambiguity by supposition' was introduced, as far as I know, by Fillmore (1966:225) in his description of the semantic structure of *come*.

Finally, it should be noted that generality is a relative notion: *animal* is more general than *monkey,* but *monkey* is still unspecific with respect to the various kinds of monkeys there are.

5.2. Some examples from Empson's *Seven types*

The distinctions made above between inherent polysemy on the one hand and vagueness and generality on the other hand are a necessary prerequisite for the description of the meaning of lexical elements. They are also useful, I believe, in a first evaluation of the rôle a linguistic description can play in an account of contextual ambiguity, which may have its source in a variety of factors that are different from the linguistic point of view.

For an illustration of this, consider the comments by Empson (1965: 68 ff.) on the following lines from Johnson's poem *The vanity of human wishes*:

> What murdered Wentworth, and what exiled Hyde,
> By kings protected, and to kings allied?
> What but their wish indulged in courts to shine,
> And power too great to keep, or to resign?

One at least of the many ambiguities Empson finds in these lines is clearly grammatical; it concerns an ambiguity of scope in line three. This line can be read as

> 'their wish to shine / indulged in courts'

or as

> 'their wish to shine in courts / indulged'

or even as

> 'their wish to shine indulged / in courts',

to disregard for the moment the possibility that the order of words and the metrical structure suggest one meaning as against another.

A second ambiguity concerns the absence of an overt Agent of 'indulged' in the same line. In the context, the consequence of this is that the implication can either be that the two men mentioned in the first line, themselves indulged their wish to 'shine', or that their wish to shine was indulged by others, in particular, by the people they were surrounded with 'in courts'.

Thirdly — I still follow Empson's comments — when we read line three as 'their wish to shine / indulged in courts', it can mean 'their wish to shine, indulged in courts on this or that occasion' or it can mean 'their wish to shine, indulged in courts as usual', with the implication that such a thing is bound to happen to anybody in those surroundings. This is a reflection of the fact that the verbal form *indulged* can be taken as Temporal or as General.

A lexical ambiguity presents itself in line two. Wentworth and Hyde can be 'allied to kings' by marriage, or they can belong to the class of people that have firmly established relationships with kings in a number of ways, in which case it means something like 'of a similar species to' (Empson 1965:68), or they can be allied to kings by some specific treaty or agreement. Both 'protected' and 'allied', it should be noted, are furthermore ambiguous in the sense that they may be taken as Adjectival or as Verbal.

The foregoing ambiguities, then, are connected with various degrees of grammatical neutralization and lexical polysemy. An ambiguity that has its source rather in a lack of specification presents itself in line four: 'power too great to keep, or to resign'. The implication of 'power too great to keep' may be either that Wentworth and Hyde were unable to handle the kind of power they had acquired, or, that they found themselves endowed with the kind of power that is too great for anybody to live with. Secondly, 'power too great to resign' could imply: (i) they had acquired a kind of power they were not willing to give up, (ii) they had acquired the kind of power that nobody would give up willingly, (iii) they actually tried to resign the power they had acquired, but the very fact that they tried to escape the entanglements they found themselves in was the cause of their downfall, since their power proved too great to (be) resign(ed).

Notice, further, that in line two the complement phrase 'by kings protected' will here be readily interpreted — though not necessarily, I believe — as 'once protected by kings' or even as '*though* they were protected by kings'. In itself, the phrase is neutral, and in the context of another poem it might just as well be interpreted as '*since* they were protected by kings', that is, as causal rather than adversative. If the third line were not clearly intended as an answer to the question posed in the first, the latter interpretation would also be quite possible in this context.

Though it is indeed difficult to draw a sharp line between 'inherent' ambiguity and mere lack of specification, it can be seen that, already, in these four lines of poetry, ambiguities are involved that are different kinds from the viewpoint of a linguistic description.

It should be noted that what I here call 'kinds' of ambiguity — lexical or grammatical; homonymy, polysemy, or mere neutrality, or vagueness — is completely different from what Empson refers to as 'types' of ambiguity. Empson's classification of types of ambiguity is made from the point of view

of their communicative effects, and their contribution to the textual structure. Secondly, many of the ambiguities treated in his book involve factors
that are hard to evaluate linguistically, such as: levels of ability in compre-
hension, degrees of sensitivity – and of ingenuity –, and knowledge of
historical background; allegory, allusions, and other forms of simultaneous
reference to more than one universe of discourse[8]; etymology and sound
symbolism; and also the intentions of the poet. Apart from its other merits,
Empson's book is therefore an excellent illustration of the fact that ambiguities in the general sense of 'possible alternative interpretations' have their
source not only in lack of contextual specification, or the complexity of the
discourse, but will also have to be explained by the complexity of the presuppositions with which the reader approaches a text.

   Still, I believe that it would be premature to conclude from this that
Empson's examples are unfit to serve as illustrations of the ambiguity problem from the point of view of the linguistic description of sentences. In almost
any chapter, the 'types' of ambiguity are illustrated with fragments where the
source of these ambiguities ranges from grammatical homonymy to mere
vagueness. A linguistic dissection of both the fragments and his comments is,
as I have found, quite a useful exercise, and it also opens one's eyes to the
possibilities for a linguistic contribution to the analysis of literary texts.

   A second reason why a linguistic study of Empson's book is not at all un-
rewarding, is that it now and then confirms the suspicion that an ambiguity
which, in terms of lexical or grammatical analysis, should present the reader
with a clear-cut either-or choice, can, in a particular context, make much less
difference than would be expected. In the lines quoted above, this is the case
in line three, where the ambiguities of scope give rise to different nuances of
the same message rather than to totally different meanings. Similarly, it is
hard to decide, and moreover does not seem to make much difference,
whether 'protected' and 'allied' in line two have a more Adjectival or a more
Verbal meaning. And such neutralizations are not necessarily brought about by
poetic contexts only.

---

[8] A description of sentences alone can only account for these kinds of ambiguity
very inadequately, if at all. Whether or not, for instance, a sentence like *This tree has
too many branches* is understood literally or non-literally is impossible to decide if one
does not know the speaker's intentions or the universe of discourse, gardening or
writing transformational grammars. Cf. Reddy (1969), for some illuminating remarks on
the implausibility of the view that metaphor can be approached in terms of sentence-
internal deviance or without taking reference into account.

5.3. Homonymy, idiom, and sense relations

5.3.1. *Homonymy*

The opposite case to generality or vagueness as a possible source of ambiguity, is homonymy. I will regard a lexical element as homonymous when its different senses have no relevant components in common: *bank* 'of a river' and *bank* 'place to deposit money'[9].

This distinction, it should be admitted, draws heavily upon some presupposed awareness of relatedness between senses, and upon the description of these relationships. It is, therefore, not at all an unambiguous criterion. There are crude cases of homonymy, like *bank* and *bank*, above, or *swallow* 'to engulf' and *swallow* 'kind of bird', but it can be disputed whether *beat* 'to hit' and *beat* 'to defeat' are unrelated senses or not. This may be the reason why the usefulness of the distinction between homonymy and polysemy has been questioned by some authors[10], and rejected by others.

Weinreich (1966b:402) criticizes the lexical descriptions as proposed in Katz and Fodor (1964) for not guaranteeing a distinction between 'lexicologically interesting polysemy' and 'fortuitous homonymy'. The meanings $ball_1$ 'social dancing', $ball_2$ 'object having globular shape', and $ball_3$ 'missile', for instance, are given in their article (p. 507) as three different senses of one and the same element *ball*, though it would appear that $ball_1$ has little in common with $ball_2$ or $ball_3$.

Against this charge, Katz (1967:147 ff.) has argued that there is no simple dichotomy between the presence and the absence of similarity in meaning, but that there is a range of similarity in meaning, whose limiting cases are, on the one hand: synonymy, and on the other: 'complete difference in meaning'.

It can be granted, I think, that the dichotomy is not simple, and that it can hardly be decided offhand whether the potential ambiguity of *beat* in the sentence

(1) They beat their opponents

is an instance of homonymy or an instance of polysemy. The problem is rather whether the distinction is useful, and whether it can be handled as a

---

[9] Following Reichling (1969[5]:43-4); also Weinreich (1966a:179): 'We would like to propose the term '(synchronic) homonymy' for pairs or sets of signs having no element of their designata in common'.

[10] Cf. Bolinger (1961b:14, fn. 1): 'It does not really matter whether we speak of the same word with different meanings, or view the form [the example discussed is the adjective *light*] as two homonyms – the same arbitrary selection is present in *It's too rough* meaning 'It's too hard' or 'It's not smooth enough'.'

structural principle in the making of a lexicon. Katz assumes that the degree of similarity between the senses of lexical elements will follow automatically from their description in terms of Markers, systematic sense components that featurize the sense of a lexical element and at the same time define relationships with and oppositions to other senses. Since these Markers — such as (Animate), (Human), (Physical Object) — are furthermore hierarchically ordered by redundancy rules (Katz 1966:229 ff.), the degree of similarity between senses would then depend on the number of Markers shared and on their relative position in the hierarchy. *Ball*$_1$ 'social dancing' shares less Markers with *ball*$_2$ 'object of globular shape' and *ball*$_3$ 'missile' than the latter two senses share mutually, and the degree of similarity between *ball*$_1$ and *ball*$_{2,3}$ is accordingly smaller than the degree of similarity between *ball*$_2$ and *ball*$_3$.

This proposal has some initial attractiveness, but I doubt whether it works satisfactorily. Counting the Markers and observing their hierarchy, it would appear that *ball* 'social dancing' and *ball* 'missile' share less Markers than *crown* 'attribute of kings' and *crown* 'coin' do, since the latter two are both (+Physical Object). But it is not at all convincing that the similarity in meaning between *crown*$_1$ and *crown*$_2$ is significantly greater than the similarity between *ball*$_1$ and *ball*$_2$. In Katz's analysis, this would be the case by definition, which is a reason to doubt the overall relevance of the definition of relationships between senses in terms of Markers.

One rather obvious reason why this implicit definition of degrees of similarity in meanings entails problems is the emphasis on conceptual sense components rather than on senses, or, perhaps, the choice of sense components. To quote once more the now somewhat worn out example of *bachelor*, it would appear that the sense 'young fur seal when without a mate at breeding time' and the sense 'adult male who has never married' are related by a feature 'without a partner of the other sex'. In the revised representation of the four senses of *bachelor* given in Katz (1966:155), this relationship does not appear at all. The two senses mentioned are related inasfar as they are the only ones that share the Marker (Male), but the sense 'young fur seal' is distinct because it is the only one of the four senses listed that has the hierarchically higher Marker (Animal) where the others have (Human).

It cannot be denied that the description of sense relations involves many difficulties, some of which I will return to below. For the moment, I will assume that elements like *swallow* 'to engulf' and *swallow* 'kind of bird', *bank* 'of a river' and *bank* 'place to deposit money', *ball* 'social dancing' and *ball* 'object of globular shape' are not to be represented in the lexicon as polysemous elements with distinct but still related senses, but as two different elements in each case, which happen to have the same phonological form[11].

As is the case with grammatical homonymy, the use of a lexically homo-nymous word in the context of a sentence where both meanings could be present, and the use of that sentence in a context where both interpretations are possible, will have a communicative effect that is known as punning, and can be explained by the high diversity of meaning. But we cannot say, con-versely, that the degree of diversity of interpretation of an ambiguous sen-tence in actual use is a criterion for the degree of diversity of its inherent content. In a sentence like

(2) This is a very old shoe

spoken in the context of an exhibition of objects found in a Phoenician grave, *old* might be taken to mean 'not new' as well as 'dating from early times'. Though these two senses of *old* are more related than the two senses of *port* in the example

(3) The soldiers took the port at night

the communicative effect of both ambiguities can be quite similar. The degree of surprise, misunderstanding, or success, will depend as much on the context and the situation as on the inherent diversity of meaning. The deliberate play on unrelated meanings will — as a rule — ensure the communicative effect more readily, which might explain why punning on homonyms is not always regarded as a very elevated form of wit[12].

5.3.2. *Idiom*

Thus far, I have tried to demonstrate that inherent polysemy of lexical elements will lie between generality on the one hand and homonymy on the

---

[11] McCawley (1968b:581) observes that discussions of homonymy often betray a pre-occupation with phonological identity rather than with sense relations. This may be true, but it is hard to see how phonological identity could be omitted in the definition of homonymous lexical elements. Some of the familiar types of word play in advertising for instance, have no other basis than the phonological identity of semantically un-related lexical elements.

[12] Godel (1948:196) has already noted that 'interpretational diversity' is not in one-to-one correspondence with 'inherent diversity of meaning'. Though contextual ambig-uity has not been my primary concern here, it is a safe assumption that equivocation and misunderstandings in actual speech will be caused more often by vagueness, gen-erality, or closely related senses of lexical elements than by homonymy.

other, and that the term polysemous can be restricted to lexical elements that have distinct but related senses.

Idiomatic expressions – and idiomaticity in general – are a test case both for the question of relatedness between senses, and for the problem of how these relationships can be described.

Following current definitions[13], an idiomatic expression will be viewed here as an expression the meaning of which cannot, except at the cost of artificiality, be described as a compositional function of the meanings of its component parts and the structure of the expression. Familiar examples of 'idioms' are:

compounds of the type *sweetheart, blackmail*;

adjective-noun constructions of the type *hot potato, red herring*;

irreversible binomials[14] of the type *pins and needles*;

phrases of the type *to kick the bucket, to bury the hatchet*.

For generative descriptions, idioms offer a number of difficulties, the main one being that they are semantically highly irregular, though, more often than not, regular phonologically and grammatically. Further, their grammatical potential is often defective, but in an unpredictable way. One apparent regularity in this connection is that the idiomatic relation between an adjective and a noun is broken when the adjective is used in the predicative position: **this potato is hot, *this herring is red*. It should be kept in mind, however, that the ingenuity of native speakers ought not to be underrated. It is quite possible that somebody might say *this potato is too hot for me* and still use the expression in its idiomatic sense. Secondly, grammatical defectiveness is not just a feature of complete idioms. It is a feature of adjectives in general that in some of their contextually more specialized senses they will rarely be found in the predicative position: *he is a good friend* / **this friend is good*[15].

Various degrees of idiomaticity in adjective-noun constructions are illustrated by Weinreich (1969) by the following triplet:

(4) blind man   'man who cannot see'
(5) blind alley   'alley without an exit'
(6) blind date   'date with somebody whose identity is not known be-
                     forehand'

---

[13] For a survey of different treatments of idiom, and for further references, see Weinreich (1969).

[14] Cf. Malkiel (1959).

[15] Though this rule works as a rule of thumb, there are many irregularities involved: see Bolinger (1968, *passim*).

In the first phrase, the degree of contextual determination of *blind* is low; this is called by Weinreich a free construction. In the second phrase, the degree of contextual determination is higher: *blind* here has the sense 'without an exit', and there is only a restricted number of elements with which it can co-occur in that sense; this is called by Weinreich a phraseological unit. In the third phrase, the degree of contextual determination is still higher, since specialized senses of both elements are involved: *blind* in the sense of 'identity unknown beforehand' and *date* in the sense of 'somebody with whom one has an assignation'. The sense of 'identity unknown beforehand' is to be viewed as a contextual specialization of *blind* that is completely and uniquely determined by its occurrence with *date*: expressions like **blind assignation* cannot be formed at will, and their interpretation would require special circumstances (Weinreich 1969:41).

Dutch counterparts of the three types listed above would be:

(7) blinde man, Eng. blind man
    ('man who cannot see')
(8) blinde steeg, Eng. blind alley
    ('alley without an exit')
(9) blinde vink, Eng. *blind finch
    ('veal olive')

In Weinreich's view, an idiomatic expression is potentially ambiguous as long as its grammatical structure is not irregular and its constituents are not unique: these conditions rule out the potential ambiguity of expressions like *blow to kingdom come* or *spic and span*. Thus, *blind date* cán also mean 'somebody with whom one has an assignation and who cannot see' if we accept that *date* can be (+Animate) in other contexts as well, and Du. *blinde vink* cán also mean 'finch that cannot see'. Though this is true in principle, it would appear that a distinction should be made here. There are cases where the idiomatic and the non-idiomatic sense of a construction exhibit a — perhaps in many cases tenuous — relationship that one could be made aware of in special circumstances, as for instance in *pins and needles*. There are other cases where the semantic relationship between the idiomatic and the non-idiomatic sense of a construction in Weinreich's own terms should rather be called 'fortuitous homonymy'. The phrase *blinde vink* in Dutch potentially has two meanings, but there is hardly any relationship between the sense 'finch that cannot see' and the sense 'veal olive' that any native speaker will be aware of.

5.3.3. *Sense relations*

I will now try to survey some other senses of Dutch *blind*, their relationships, and the potential ambiguities of the phrases in which it occurs in its different senses. We have

1. blinde man, Eng.   blind man
   ('man who cannot see')
2. blinde woede,   blind rage
   ('terrible rage')
3. blind vertrouwen,   blind faith
   ('unquestioning faith')
4. blinde klip,   *blind cliff
   ('submerged rock')
5. blind vliegen,   to fly blind
   ('to fly by compass and radio only')
6. blinde steeg,   blind alley
   ('alley without an exit')
7. blinde pijp,   *blind pipe
   ('organ pipe that only serves as an ornament')
8. blinde kaart,   *blind map
   ('blank map')
9. blinde muur,   *blind wall
   ('blank wall')
10. blinde passagier,   *blind passenger
    ('stowaway')
11. blinde vink,   *blind finch
    ('veal olive')

There are two senses of *blind* in the above list that are related quite conspicuously: *blind* in 1, 'unable to see' and *blind* in 4 and 10, 'not to be seen, hidden', 'unnoticed'. If we represent the semantic structure of *blind* in 1 as 'x cannot see (y)', where y is an implicit Object, the sense of *blind* in 4 and 10 can be represented as the Passive equivalent of that structure: 'y cannot be seen (by x)', where x is an implicit Subject.

To this, the following should be added. Firstly, the representation of the sense of *blind* in 1 as 'x cannot see (y)' is slightly simplified. There is a presupposition connected with the sense of *blind* in 1: 'unable to see, though belonging to the class of animate beings that are supposed to be able to see', or, 'deprived of the faculty of sight'. An organism that by definition does not have the perceptual abilities we refer to as 'sight', for instance, a plant, will not be called *blind*. Another facet of the sense of *blind* in 1 not represented in the semantic structure given above is that in the phrase *blinde man*, 'blind man', the attributive Adjective will be taken to express an inherent relation;

that is, the relationship between *blind* and *man* expressed is (−Temporal)[16].
In other words, with regard to the one semantic structure by which the senses
of *blind* in 1 and in 4 and 10 can be related, the sense of *blind* in 1 is specialized on at least two counts.

The same is true, in fact, of the senses of *blind* in 4 and 10. In both cases,
there is a specialized sense, 'hidden' and 'gone unnoticed' respectively.
Furthermore, the phrase *blinde klip* has a certain expressiveness which its
paraphrase 'cliff that cannot be seen' or 'submerged rock' has not.

Of the other relationships between the senses of *blind* that can be pointed
out, much the same can be said: there are regularities to be stated, but a number of irregularities are involved as well.

If we start once more from the structure 'x cannot see (y)', the sense of
blind in 2 and 3 can be related to this representation by addition of a feature
(+Causative) and (+Resultative): *blinde woede*, 'blind rage' can be interpreted
as 'a rage that makes you blind', but there is a specialization involved that
should be rather paraphrased as 'making you act without using your own
capacities of judgement'. In 5, *blind vliegen*, 'to fly blind', *blind* can be interpreted as 'deprived of certain possibilities of perception, or of orientation'.
One regularity involved here is that in 5 the relation between *blind* and the
Subject of *vliegen*, 'to fly', is (+Temporal), whereas in 1, where *blind* is in the
Attributive position, the relation expressed is (−Temporal).

Next, consider the sense 'without an exit' of *blind* in 6. Though it is perhaps possible to relate this to 'not being able to see' through 'not having eyes'
or 'not having a connection with the outside world', I would say that we here
have a highly specialized sense of *blind* as compared to its sense in 1. For
blind in 7, the same is true: it is hard to state any regular relationship between
'not being able to see' and 'only serving as an ornament'[17].

The senses of *blind* in 8 and 9, English 'blank', are clearly related to its
sense in 4 and 10:'y cannot be seen' → 'nothing is to be seen on y'. Furthermore, the presupposition connected with *blind* in 1, which can be shortened
to 'abnormal' is preserved also: *a blank map* is not a normal map, but a map
that lacks something. But here, a certain arbitrariness creeps in. *Een blinde
kaart*, 'a blank map' can indeed be interpreted as 'a map on which you cannot
see what you expect to be there', but to some native speakers of Dutch it
appears to mean 'a map which looks like something without eyes'.

I believe that the problem we have here is not unlike the problem of the re-

---

[16] But here too, there are exceptions; the blindness of *blind puppies*, 'blinde jongen'
will normally be (+Temporal), though, strictly speaking, the phrase is ambiguous.

[17] Perhaps by metaphorical extension: *blind* 'unseeing' → 'not serving its purpose'.

lationships between grammatical structures commented on in chapter 4, above: we can point to a semantic structure underlying the various senses of *blind*, and in some cases the relationships between these senses can be stated with the use of such categorial features as (Active), (Passive), (Causative), but there still remains a gap, larger in some cases than in others, between these underlying structures and the senses of *blind*.

As far as the potential ambiguity of the phrases listed above is concerned, these are – as in the case of potential grammatical ambiguities – restricted by quite a number of factors.
(i) Features of the Nouns with which the Adjective *blind* occurs. The idiom *blinde passagier* '*blind passenger' is potentially ambiguous as between the interpretations 'stowaway' and 'passenger who cannot see', but the phrase *blinde kaart* 'blank map', can hardly be interpreted as 'map that cannot see', since *kaart* 'map' is (−Animate). Similarly, *blinde klip* 'submerged rock' can only be understood metaphorically as 'rock that cannot see'.
(ii) Grammatical context. In most examples, *blind* will only, or preferably, occur in attributive position. If one wants to avoid terms like 'impossible' or 'ungrammatical' one can say that in many cases the use of *blind* in a certain sensè in Predicative position requires more context or more presuppositons. Compare:

    1a. Deze man is blind
       ('This man is blind')
    4a. ?Deze klip is blind
       (*'This cliff is blind')
    6a. ?Deze steeg is blind
       ('This alley is blind')
  10a. *Deze passagier is blind
       (*'This passenger is blind')

The senses of *blind* that are least likely to occur in the predicative position are the most idiomatic ones.
(iii) Restricted productivity. Many of the senses of *blind* listed above can only occur with a restricted set of elements. *Blind enthusiasme* ('blind enthusiasm') as an analogy of 3 *blind vertrouwen* ('unquestioning faith') is understandable, but *blinde ijsberg* ('blind iceberg') as an analogy of 4 *blinde klip* ('submerged rock'), though perhaps understandable, is certainly uncommon. Here too, the most idiomatic senses are the least productive ones: *blinde gast* ('blind guest') for 'guest who does not pay' as an analogy of 10 *blinde passagier* ('stowaway') is strange.

The potential ambiguities of these phrases, then, are restricted to a small number of privileged contexts. The realization of these potential ambiguities will, of course, be further constrained by various unpredictable features of the larger contexts in which these phrases occur.

Let us now for a moment return to the question of the relations between the various senses of *blind*. As we saw, even in those cases where these relationships are quite obvious, as in 1 'unable to see' and in 4 'not to be seen', certain irregularities and specializations are involved, and problems increase enormously in the case of completely idiomatic expressions such as 11 *blinde vink*. Without consulting a specialized dictionary where such expressions are explained, one is unable to make any sensible comment on the semantic relation between *blind* in *blinde man* and *blind* in *blinde vink* 'veal olive'. Therefore, it is understandable that Weinreich (o.c. p. 77) flatly denies the possibility of formulating rules of sense derivation; they would amount to an artificial 'explanation' a posteriori. But the example he gives — *to eat crow* in the sense 'to accept what one has fought against' — is quite extreme. The Dutch idiomatic expression *blinde passagier* 'stowaway', seems clearly explainable in terms of a connection with *blind* 'not to be seen'; what remains arbitrary here is that in this sense, *blind* is conventionally combined with only one (+Animate) Noun, and that the phrase then has the meaning 'stowaway' and not just *any* 'passenger that cannot be seen'. Still, the dilemma remains that the mechanism by which such idiomatic expressions are coined must be quite productive, though its outcomes can be arbitrary. This apparently is the reason why Bolinger (1965a:567) has required that a semantic theory must at least be able to say *something* about such processes; and in my opinion this requirement is even more compelling in those cases where sense relationships are more regular than in the case of idioms. It can be questioned whether we are justified in speaking of 'rules' when the outcome of a sense shift is to an extent unpredictable, and unpredictable features of language use will intervene. But it cannot be denied that there is a kind of creativity at work that is somehow based on the system of the language, and that some senses of lexical elements are related to each other quite regularly.

The viewpoint that the lexicon is the set of basic irregularities, therefore, in my opinion cannot be interpreted to mean 'the lexicon is just the set of all the senses of a lexical element', for two reasons. The first reason is that even among those senses that will have to be listed for the sake of descriptive adequacy, there are relationships that will have to be stated as well. The second, and more important reason is that there are possible interpretations of lexical elements that need not be listed at all as so many different 'senses', but are to be substracted from the lexicon and to be explained by rules of semantic interpretation. In the following paragraph, I will therefore argue that the views on polysemy and ambiguity as put forward by Katz and Fodor in their 1964 article and by Katz in subsequent publications, are untenable.

5.4. Katz and Fodor on ambiguity and polysemy

5.4.1. *Ambiguity as a heuristic device*

The solution to the ambiguity and polysemy problem as proposed in the first formalized an explicit schema for a generative semantic theory in Katz and Fodor (1964), Katz (1966), and Katz (1967) is essentially the following. The goal of a semantic theory in their view is to list the senses a lexical element can have in the context of different sentences, to give a description of the semantic structure of these senses (in particular, the conceptual structure; see Katz (1966:154)) in terms of language-systematic Markers, idiosyncratic Distinguishers, and selectional restrictions, and to devise projection rules – rules that form the contents of sentences – by which the appropriate senses of lexical elements are selected and combined in the grammatical structures in which they occur.

In their evaluation of the best way to describe meanings, Katz and Fodor make quite extensive use of the following criteria: (i) the detection of ambiguities a native speaker must be regarded as capable of, (ii) the resolution of ambiguities ('disambiguation') a native speaker must be regarded as capable of. Thus, the sentence

(10) There is no school any more

(Katz 1966:158 ff., Katz 1967:136) can mean 'there are no more teaching sessions' or 'the building is no longer there', but the sentence

(11) The school burnt down

rules out the interpretation 'teaching sessions'. Similarly, we may expect that the sentence

(12) They had an appointment at the bank

is ambiguous as between the interpretations 'place for depositing money' and 'side of a river' of *bank*, but that the sentence

(13) The bank was robbed twice this year

is not.

Thus, when a lexical element is polysemous in the sense that in one isolated sentence it has a sense A and in another isolated sentence it has a sense

B, and in some sentences either A or B, this should have its reflection in the lexicon: A and B are different senses of that lexical element. Or, in general: when a lexical element appears to have *n* different senses, it accordingly has *n* dictionary entries (the term dictionary is used in Katz and Fodor 1964 for what I call here the lexicon). Compare Katz and Fodor (1964:493): 'A dictionary entry is a characterization of *every* sense a lexical element can bear in any sentence' (authors' italics – JGK). Thus, the effect of the projection rules must be to select the appropriate sense of each lexical element in a sentence'. Compare also Katz (1966:155): 'Each distinct reading in a dictionary entry for a word represents one of the word's senses'.

To avoid the unlimited accumulation of different senses, Katz and Fodor (1964:486 ff.; see also Katz 1967:135 ff.) make a distinction between those ambiguities that are detected or resolved on the level of the isolated sentence by 'competence' and those ambiguities that might be detected or resolved in a certain context or situation ('setting', see Katz and Fodor 1964:486) by extra-linguistic 'knowledge of the world'. The distinction between language-systematic Markers and idiosyncratic Distinguishers in their sense descriptions reflects, among other things, this difference between a native speaker's capacity of automatic selection of the appropriate sense of a lexical element on the one hand, the sentence-internal disambiguation, as against possible disambiguation by 'knowledge of the world' on the other hand.

5.4.2. Disambiguation

It can be shown – and it has been demonstrated conclusively in Bolinger (1965a) – that this basis for distinguishing between Markers and Distinguishers is a delicate one[18]. To quote one of Bolinger's examples, if native speakers automatically exclude the sense of *bachelor* 'knight serving under the standard of another knight' in the sentence *The old bachelor finally died*, we can say with Katz and Fodor that (Young) is a Marker in this sense of bachelor. But for other speakers, the sentence *That peasant is a happy bachelor* will also be unambiguous because *knight* is incompatible with *peasant*, so that some Marker for 'Status' will have to be added to the sense description of *bachelor*. Relying on the native speaker's supposed capacity for automatic, sentence-internal disambiguation of lexical elements, in order to decide which sense components should be represented as Markers and which as Distinguishers, will lead to an endless transference of features from

---

[18] There are other reasons why this distinction rests on precarious grounds: cf. the criticisms in Bolinger (1965a:558-62 and 568-9), and in Weinreich (1966b:405-6).

Distinguisher status to Marker status until the Distinguisher material is exhausted.

If we view semantic features such as the Markers and Distinguishers of Katz and Fodor as the presuppositions that are connected with the various senses of lexical elements, it is true that some of these presuppositons are more inclusive than others, while some of them are more tied up with properties of denotata than others. But it is highly doubtful whether ambiguity can serve as a criterion in drawing the delicate boundary between semantic 'competence' and 'knowledge of the world'.

There are other reasons why the ambiguity criterion is a hazardous one. It is doubtful whether native speakers' ideal 'knowledge' of the senses of lexical elements has any sufficiently interesting correlate with their capacity to select them in isolated sentences.

Consider the following example from McKay and Bever (1967:199-200). The test subjects were presented with the sentence

(14) The marine captain liked his new position

The consensus was that this sentence could be interpreted in two ways: (i) the marine captain liked the new position of his ship, (ii) the marine captain liked his new rank. This ambiguity reflects a polysemy of the word *position*, that may be roughly represented as (i) Position, place with respect to other entities, (+Local), (ii) Position, place with respect to other people, (−Local), Rank, ...,. That native speakers will select the above mentioned interpretations of sentence (14) is understandable in view of the fact that these two interpretations will be the most readily associated with the phrase *marine captain*; that is, even sentences in isolation will evoke a context (to a certain extent). But the possible ambiguities of the sentence (14) are not at all exhausted by these two interpretations. The marine captain may have broken his leg six weeks ago, and just have been told by the doctor that he now has permission to sit upright in a chair instead of lying in his bed. The marine captain likes his new (+Local) position. He may also be a regular contributor to a journal of ballistic techniques and involved in a heated and prolonged discusssion with a colleague. On writing his next-to-last rejoinder, he realizes that his original standpoint has changed in the course of the discussion. And since he feels that it has not only changed but also improved, the marine captain likes his new (−Local) position (in the debate).

There may be many more positions our marine captain may find himself in and be pleased with. All these interpretations are interpretations a native speaker should be capable of if he knows his language and a few other things. If he thinks hard enough, he probably will be so capable, even when he has no more to go on than an isolated sentence. But a dilemma presents itself here. Either 'automatic detection and resolution of ambiguities', as Katz and Fodor use the expression, is simply part of the ideal native speaker's supposed semantic competence, and does not refer to any actual interpretative activity at all, or, 'automatic detection and resolution of ambiguities' *does* refer to the actual interpretation of isolated sentences. In that case, several other factors will be involved, as I have tried to show above, so that 'actual disambiguation' can no longer be invoked as something upon which a definition of ideal 'competence' can be based.

I think that Katz and Fodor (see also the repeated statement in Katz 1967: 135) confuse the issue by the assumption that there are two strictly separable forms of 'disambiguation'. In their view, disambiguation either takes place on the basis of 'competence', where it is synonymous with 'automatic sentence-internal selection of not incompatible senses'; or disambiguation is a matter of 'performance' and takes place on the basis of knowledge of the world, or setting, the context and the situation surrounding the utterance token. This is a pseudo-dualism. The selection of non-incompatible senses should be viewed as *always* a matter of performance, or rather, of 'interpretation', based on a lot of factors of which competence in the sense of 'knowledge of the semantic structure of the language' is only one. What is referred to by Katz as a distinction between competence and performance *is* in fact a distinction between 'more or less obligatory disambiguation' and 'more or less optional disambiguation'. It is artificial to assume that the way in which a native speaker resolves the potential ambiguity of *colourful* as between the senses 'having a variety of colours' and 'vivid' in the sentence

(15) He told us a quite colourful story

is totally different from the way he resolves the potential ambiguity in the sequence

(16) He told us a story. It was quite colourful.

The difference here resides in the difference between the linguistic description of sentences and of discourses[19], but not in what is put to use by native speakers in disambiguation.

The sentence-internal disambiguation Katz and Fodor put so much weight on is just one instance of contextual disambiguation in general; and on the level of the sentence as well, in many cases there will be involved degrees of probability or oddness rather than absolute either-or choices. For some people, *ball* in

[19] For footnote, see next page.

(17) She opened the ball with a pen-knife

might have all three senses of *ball*: 'object of globular shape', 'missile', or 'social dancing'; for others, it might not. This is the same problem as the one that arose in chapter 4, p. 112 above, in connection with sentences like

(18) Old men and babies were left at the village
(19) John loves old port and coca cola
(20) He hit the man with Sheila

The relation between potential and actual ambiguity is not at all clear in such sentences, and for a linguistic description the question will often be undecidable. The problems inherent in the exclusive focussing on sentences in isolation, in connection with a problem like ambiguity, have become really grotesque in the K/F schema for a semantic theory.

5.4.3. *Infinite polysemy*

No less a problem is presented by the assumption that for the number of senses of a lexical element to be listed in the lexicon we can rely upon existing dictionaries (Katz and Fodor 1964, *passim*, see especially p. 502, and compare also the quotation from p. 493 given earlier, p. 134 above). It is a conspicuous feature of dictionaries[20] that they tend to list as separate 'senses' of a lexical element almost any interpretation it might have in a particular context, and more often than not do this by adding the context in which the interpretation referred to is attested. Katz and Fodor (p. 500) seem to be quite happy with this situation: 'Where the conventional dictionary, by using such devices as 'of ...' tells us what a word means in certain combinations, our reconstruction must do so systematically', that is, by adding a new sense together with a selectional restriction. This procedure leads to a unwarrantable loss of economy, and removes the opportunity of indicating which 'senses' are to be viewed as contextual specializations, and which are to be viewed as senses that have indeed to be listed.

---

[19] I will not consider here Katz and Fodor's parenthetical definition of discourse as 'in the great majority of cases' (490-1) a matter of *and*-conjunction between sentences. This is either a tautology (formally speaking, all discourses can be viewed as sets of linearly ordered sentences) or it is an overly optimistic view on the intricacies of semantic discourse relations. The latter also applies to their remark added in fn. 11, p. 490: '(...)given a theory of semantic interpretation [of sentences in isolation] it is unclear how much is left for a theory of setting selection to explain'.

[20] For a critique of this tendency in the semantic descriptions in conventional dictionaries, see Weinreich 1964.

Both the extensive use of ambiguity and disambiguation as a heuristic device in lexical description, and the assumption that the senses given in existing dictionaries can be transferred to the lexicon as part of a linguistic description, requiring only to be more systematically represented[21], have led to a justified criticism by Weinreich (1966b:411) that the principles adopted in the semantic theory of Katz and Fodor are bound to lead to infinite polysemy. Contextual specializations as they are faithfully encoded by the dictionary makers in the form 'x means A_1 but it means A_2 when said of p' have no end, and ambiguities are also quite unlimited. That this is an inherent problem of their proposals has been categorically denied by Katz (1967:114): 'The dictionary [lexicon] is one aspect of the speaker's semantic competence, and since speakers are only equipped with finite brains, the mechanism reconstructed by a dictionary can, in principle, store only finitely many bits of information about the lexical characterization of a particular item'.

I believe that here – as on many other pages of this article – Katz misses the point of the criticism he is answering. What is worrying about the principles laid out in Katz and Fodor (1964) and Katz (1966), is that they can lead to a real proliferation of different senses. The issue is hardly whether this accumulation of senses is to be viewed as finite or infinite in the mathematical sense; the issue is that the number of distinct senses is too large. It may very well be that it was never the intention to list *all* contextual specializations of lexical elements, but as long as we are to believe that the number of senses is roughly the number of senses to be found in Webster's Third, there is hardly anything by which this claim can be substantiated[22].

Further, another problematic aspect of their view of a semantic theory becomes visible in the above quotation: the view that a lexicon is a systematic

---

[21] On one occasion, in his analysis of the meaning of the adjective *good* (Katz 1964; Katz 1966:283 ff.), Katz has defended exactly the opposite position, namely that the meaning of *good* is not to be viewed as an independent attribute, but as 'a function which operates on other meanings' (1966:312). It is doubtful, however, whether the reduction of the inherent meaning of *good* can be pushed as far as Katz does. For a more moderate view, cf. Ziff (1964:200 ff.).

[22] On this point, Weinreich's criticisms have been rebutted by McCawley (1968b:584) who notes that there is no reason to assume that Katz and Fodor would list two distinct senses of *eat*, *eat_j* and *eat_k*, because it will be understood slightly differently in the sentences *I eat bread* and *I eat soup*. It may be true that this example is somewhat far-fetched, but it cannot be denied that the principles outlined in Katz and Fodor (1964) for arriving at adequate semantic representations of lexical elements would lead to an accumulation of distinct senses. The 'desire for systematic economy' is mentioned (e.g. on p. 499), but it is nowhere apparent how polysemy could actually be reduced.

storage of 'finitely many bits of information'[23]. It is not the primary goal of a semantic theory to give a systematic representation of the various senses of lexical elements, and it is certainly not its only goal. What a semantic theory should be concerned with, first of all, is to try to define some structure among these senses by formulating the principles by which these senses are related; and to decide to what extent these same principles are operative in the formation of the content of a sentence and in its further specifications in the context.

To give some simple examples, it is not so very interesting whether or not a native speaker 'knows' that *star* can mean 'asterisk' as well as 'planet' and 'highly publicized performer, leading actor'. What is interesting is that he knows a rule which says that elements like *star* can be used in the sense of 'a conventional representation of ——'; some of these uses have been conventionalized and have therefore found their way into our dictionaries, others have not. It is not so very interesting whether or not a native speaker knows that *tree* can mean 'visual representation of a phrase-maker' in some contexts or for some people, and that for those people the expression *tree-pruning* can be ambiguous. What is interesting is that there is a principle by which *tree* and many other words can be used under many different circumstances to refer to 'something being alike to ——, under one of its aspects'.

Let me give another example. Among the distinct senses of the verb *zien* 'to see' listed by Dutch dictionaries there are: $zien_1$: 'being able to see, having the faculty of sight', and $zien_2$: 'being able to use this faculty on certain occasions'. $Zien_1$ is the sense of *zien* in

(21) Hij ziet scherp
('He has sharp eyes')

and $zien_2$ is the sense of *zien* in

(22) Katten zien in het donker
('Cats are able to see in the dark')

But surely, both these 'senses' of *zien* can be explained by a rule to the effect that [−Agentive] or [+Stative] verbs like *zien*, when used without an Object or Complement, acquire an Absolute sense that can be paraphrased as 'being able to ——'; and surely the 'sense' $zien_2$ is just another contextual specializa-

---

[23] Cf. also Katz and Fodor (1964:494-5): 'The dictionary is something that the speaker learns item by item, in a more or less rote fashion (...) the utilization of what is learned in learning a dictionary consists of recalling relatively independent bits of information'.

tion of the same sense of *zien* that we have in (21)[24].

It is strange that a theory that has always put much emphasis on creativity and argued that native speakers create sentences and do not just repeat sentences used before, has been supplemented — at least in its standard version — by a theory of semantic interpretation that is static and views the formation of the content of a sentence as a process in which ready-made senses with ready-made selectional restrictions are selected and combined in ready-made grammatical frameworks.

5.4.4. *'Setting'*

In this connection, it is necessary to add a comment on Katz and Fodor's view of 'setting' — the context and the situation in general in which sentences are actually used —, and on the extent to which a semantic theory should be concerned with setting. On p. 488, they write:

'(...) a theory of settings must contain a theory of semantic interpretation [of sentences in isolation] as a proper part, because the readings that a speaker attributes to a sentence in a setting are a selection from among those that the sentence has in isolation. It is clear that, *in general* (author's italics — JGK), a sentence cannot have readings in a setting which it does not have in isolation'.

This is the wrong conclusion from the right premise, and again contributes to the multiplication of the polysemy problem. The premise is that the linguistic description of the semantic structure of sentences must precede the theory of contextual and situational specification in language use. To conclude from this that the effect of 'setting' is solely selective can only mean that all different ways in which lexical elements, or sentences in general, can be understood, should be specified as such in the description of the sentence, as so many disjunctions. If we recall the example of a sentence like

(14) The marine captain liked his new position

and the various readings it could have, we would be compelled to list all these readings as readings it has in isolation, and to attribute a lot of different senses to the word *position*. But some of these readings are merely contextual specializations of the same sense of *position*: 'situation, (+Local)', and others

---

[24] A sense of *zien* that will have to be listed is the sense it has in *Hij ziet bleek*, 'He looks pale'. But this should certainly not be done without indicating at the same time that this sense of *zien* and the sense it has in *Hij ziet Piet*, 'He sees Peter', are related to each other in much the same way as the senses of *snijden*, 'to cut' in *Dit brood snijdt makkelijk*, 'This bread cuts easily', and *Hij snijdt het brood*, 'He cuts the bread'. A similar relationship as there exists between these two senses of *zien* is exhibited, of course, by the two senses of Du. *blind* 'not to be seen' and 'unable to see'.

are merely contextual specializations of *position*: 'situation, (−Local)'. Thus, the marine captain might like his new position as a full-back after having played half-back for many years, and the position of his ship might be: just its location, or its strategic position. By incorporating all these distinctions, we will burden the semantic description of the sentence, as well as the lexicon, with superfluous information.

If we take an alternative approach — as I think we should — we can define one sense of *position* roughly as 'situation, (+Local)', as far as the lexicon is concerned. But then, of course, we can no longer maintain that the interpretations of *position* in (14) and of (14) in context are a selection from among those it has in isolation. 'Situation, (+Local)' is not an interpretation, but a linguistic specification of a semantic structure that awaits further specialization. And it is the specification of such semantic structures that a description of sentences in isolation can properly deal with.

The conclusion drawn by Katz and Fodor, therefore, should be reversed. The readings of a sentence in isolation are only a subset of the readings it can have in language use. Put differently, of the readings a sentence can have in a discourse, one subset can be specified in its linguistic description — in this case, corresponding to the different inherent senses of *position*, one subset can more or less be predicted — *position* would be understood differently when the Subject of (14) is *The district's attorney* instead of *the marine captain*, and still another subset can only be guessed at — on the basis of an isolated sentence, we have no means of knowing what further specializations will be contributed by the interpretation of a sentence in discourse. What is true of grammatical structures as discussed in the foregoing chapter in connection with sentences like *He hit the man with the stick*, is no less true of the various ways in which lexical elements can be understood; there is a difference, and no small one, between definable and undefinable ambiguities.

A statement on the effect of 'setting' like the one by Katz and Fodor quoted above, is not only contradicted on every other page of Empson's *Seven types*, but can be falsified with much simpler examples than his. In the following section, I will be concerned with some of these.

5.5. Ambiguity, polysemy, and interpretation: some final examples
Consider the sentence

(23) He looked at the plane

This can mean that 'he' looked at a plane standing at an airport, or at the picture of a plane, or at a toy plane. This appears not to be a counterexample to the Katz and Fodor view, since we can say that these different interpretations

are solely a function of reference. But that would be only partially true, since
at least the interpretation 'picture of' is the result of the application of the
general and simple rule that some lexical elements can always be used and
understood to refer to 'the representation of —', without therefore being
elements that are inherently polysemous. Thus, the sentence

(24) Today I saw Richard Burton[25]

could mean that I actually saw him walking in the street, or that I saw him
walking in the street on television. And the sentence

(25) Today I saw Richard Burton at Madame Tussaud's

could mean that I met the famous star at that place, or that I contemplated
his wax figure. But we will not conclude that proper names have a sense
'somebody by the name of x' and another sense 'some kind of representation
of that somebody'. We will conclude that the rule mentioned in connection
with (23) applies here as well, and that the specific results of its application
in different contexts could not even be listed since they are, in principle,
unlimited.

There are other and less trivial examples of alternative interpretations that
do not entail a lexical element having different senses. Consider the sentences

(26) The president lost his glasses on the pavement
(27) The president is the constitutional head of the republic

In the first sentence, a natural interpretation is that *the president* refers to
some person who happens to be president, in the second sentence, a natural
interpretation is that *the president*, though still (+Referential), refers more
specifically to that person's function. When taken as (−Referential), *the president* could also refer to that function in general. Compare also

(28) The pope stepped out of the aeroplane
(29) The pope is infallible

These different interpretations can be explained by assuming that inherent to
the sense of Nouns like *president* and *pope* and Noun Phrases like *chairman of
the women's league* are a component 'somebody' and a component 'function'.
Their semantic structure can be represented as $f(x)$ where x refers to the person
and f to his function, for instance[26], but whatever representation we choose,
what it should not reflect is that such Nouns have two different senses to

---

[25] This example was taken, with slight alteration, from Reddy (1969).
[26] For footnote, see next page.

which two different entries in the lexicon correspond.

One argument for this is that the interpretations most readily associated with (26) and (28) are, after all, not excluded in (27) and (29), and that the interpretations most readily associated with (27) and (29) are not excluded in (26) and (28). One facet of the semantic structure of these Nouns will more readily be actualized in one context than in another, while in still other contexts, like

(30) The pope has declared war on the pill
(31) The president will decide on this question

it is hard to decide, and, in addition, immaterial, whether reference is made to some person or more particularly to his function. As another example, consider a sentence like

(32) You gave her the wrong answer

This sentence can be interpreted as 'the answer you gave was not the answer that is known by convention as the right solution to a certain problem'. It could also mean 'the answer you gave (in the sense of 'the solution you suggested') turned out to be the wrong answer'. Or it could mean 'the answer you gave was not quite the appropriate thing to say to her in that situation; though it was factually not wrong, it was wrong as a speech act'. In many larger contexts, I assume that it will be clear what was intended, but the conclusion that these different interpretations are to be related to different senses of *wrong* or *answer* is not a very attractive one. It is natural to conclude that *wrong* has only one sense here, that may be paraphrased as 'inappropriate with respect to —' and that, like many relative terms, it can be interpreted in a more Absolute sense in some contexts, 'wrong by convention' and in a more Relative sense in other contexts 'wrong with respect to certain circumstances or purposes'. For words like *answer*, I will assume that they can be interpreted as either 'act of —ing' or as 'the — itself'. Here too, there will be other contexts where the difference does not make itself felt clearly, for instance a sentence like

[26] Cf. Bolinger (1968:14 ff.), on the two interpretations of phrases like *an eager student* which can mean 'eager as a person' or 'eager as a student'. Bolinger proposes the terms 'referent modification' and 'reference modification' to discriminate between these two interpretations. As far as the 'generic' interpretation of sentences like (27) and (29) is concerned, I will assume, with Smith (1964:49 ff.) that positing the existence of a generic determiner the_2, homonymous with the definite determiner the_1, is not much of an explanation. Though I have no completely worked-out alternative to offer, it would appear that whether or not a phrase like *the president* in a sentence like (27) is interpreted as (+Referential) or as (−Referential), will depend on the context in many cases.

(33) His answer did not please me very much

It is my view, then, that different specifications of the compositional structure of one and the same sense that might lead to ambiguities in those cases where the context of the sentence is not decisive, are not equivalent to ambiguities that point to the existence of different senses of lexical elements, or different semantic structures of sentences. In this respect, my argument is similar to the argument adduced in the foregoing chapters in connection with grammatical analysis: there comes a point where 'ambiguity' is to be explained by rules of contextual specialization of one and the same semantic structure, rather than by positing different structures one of which is selected in the context.

The extent to which such interpretative rules are feasible is a question I will not try to decide here, and the same is to be said for the question of whether any exact boundary between inherent polysemy and other forms of ambiguity can be drawn. I will summarize two important arguments in favour of recognizing that some such boundary should be drawn: (i) economy of description, (ii) forms of neutralization that do not find an obvious explanation under the assumption that an actual either-or choice is involved[27]. As a third argument can be added (iii) the re-establishment of a connection between the semantic description of sentences in isolation and the semantic structuring of larger discourses. It is a basic assumption with many authors that an absolute distinction should be maintained between the two, but I think that on many occasions one is forced to conclude that the distinction between the rôle of sentence context and the rôle of larger contexts is much more gradual.

As a final illustration of the problems inherent in the linguistic specification of ambiguities, consider a sentence like

(34) The book gave him a lot of trouble

This sentence has at least two interpretations: 'writing the book gave him a lot of trouble', or 'the book itself gave him a lot of trouble'. An element like *book* is systematically ambiguous as between the interpretations 'production of —' and 'the product itself', and the same is true of elements like (*gramophone*)*record, story, article, sermon, lecture*[28]. Another potential ambiguity is the one between the interpretations 'physical embodiment of —' and

---

[27] Cf. also Chomsky (1970, esp. fn. 8 and 12, p. 216-7).

[28] According to McCawley (1968a:131), these two interpretations of elements like *book* can be explained by a rule of 'reification'.

Words like *sermon* and *lecture*, can also be understood in a sense that might be paraphrased as 'the reproduction of —', whereas *book* and *article* hardly can be so interpreted. It requires some effort to interpret *?I listened to his book.*

'contents of —': a book may cause trouble because of what it says, or because of the fact that it inadvertently fell on somebody's head. The latter interpretation, however, is less likely to occur when we replace *book* in (34) by *article*. So, some of the presuppositions connected with the senses of lexical elements have a less systematic impact on lexical description than others. 'Production of —', for instance, can still be understood as 'by the printers' or 'by the author' in the case of (34). But since the activities associated with producing a record are different from those associated with producing a book, 'production of —' will receive different interpretations when *book* in (34) is replaced by *record*. It remains to be seen whether the enumeration of all these presuppositions falls within the scope of a semantic theory; it would take us rather far afield.

Nor is it imperative that the different interpretations mentioned above present themselves as real alternatives in all contexts. There is nothing strange or paradoxical about the sentence

(35) The book on antique coins lies on my desk

though, strictly speaking, *on antique coins* reinforces the interpretation 'contents' of *book* and *lies on my desk* reinforces the interpretation 'physical embodiment'. The difference, that may be relevant in some contexts, is completely neutralized in other contexts. This is one criterion for distinguishing between this kind of potential ambiguity and ambiguity that has its source inherent polysemy. In a sentence like

(36) My old friend Jimmy came to see me

old friend can be interpreted as 'friend comparatively advanced in age' or 'friend of long standing'. Though there might be *persons* to whom both interpretations apply at the same time, it is difficult to think of a context where the distinction between these two *senses* of *old* would be neutralized with the effect that it would be immaterial what kind of friend was spoken about. Finally, consider the sentence

(37) The book caused uproar ˉ

I will assume that the interpretation 'production of' is ruled out here, because *caused uproar* presupposes that reference is to an existent book. The sentence then still allows for the interpretations 'contents' and 'physical embodiment' of *book*. Not that the choice is obligatory: a book could also cause uproar for both reasons, for instance with a tribe where the encoding of narratives in printed objects of a certain kind was taboo. But more important is that 'contents' and 'physical embodiment' are still only an approximation.

A book could cause uproar because its contents are obscene or obsolete, or because it was printed in capital letters with different colours, or because it stood three feet high. These are all possible interpretations of the sentence *the book caused uproar*, but not interpretations to be specified in its semantic description. We can argue over where the boundary has to be drawn, but I think we can hardly doubt that ambiguities have no end, whereas linguistic specifications have.

BIBLIOGRAPHY

Abercrombie, David a.o. (eds.)
1964   *In honour of Daniel Jones*. Papers contributed on the occasion of his
        80th birthday 12 September 1961. London, etc.
Agricola, Erhard
1968   *Syntaktische Mehrdeutigkeit (Polysyntaktizität) bei der Analyse des
        Deutschen und des Englischen*. Schriften zur Phonetik, Sprachwissen-
        schaft und Kommunikationsforschung 12. Berlin.
Anderson, John
1968a   'Ergative and nominative in English'. *JL* 4, 1-32.
1968b   'On the status of lexical formatives'. *FL* 4, 308-18.
Aristotle
        Ars rhetorica. Ed. W.D.Ross. Oxford, 1959.
        De sophisticis elenchis. Ed. W.D.Ross. Oxford, 1958.
        Topica. Ed. W.D.Ross. Oxford, 1958.

Bach, Emmon
1968   'Nouns and noun phrases'. In: Bach and Harms 1968, 91-122.
Bach, Emmon and Robert T.Harms (eds.)
1968   *Universals in linguistic theory*. New York, etc.
Bally, Charles
1944[2] *Linguistique générale et linguistique française*. Berne.
Bazell, C.E.
1949a   'On some asymmetries of the linguistic system'. *AL* 5, 139-45.
1949b   'On the problem of the morpheme'. *ArchL* 1, 1-15. Quoted from: Hamp,
        Householder, and Austerlitz 1966, 216-26.
1952   'The correspondence fallacy in structural linguistics'. In: *Studies by
        members of the English Department*, Istanbul University 3, 1-41.
        Quoted from: Hamp, Householder, and Austerlitz 1966, 271-98.
1954   'The sememe'. *Litera* 1, 17-31. Quoted from: Hamp, Householder, and
        Austerlitz 1966, 329-40.
Bendix, Edward H.
1966   *Componential analysis of general vocabulary: the semantic structure of a
        set of verbs in English, Hindi, and Japanese*. Indiana Univ. Research
        Center in Anthropology, Folklore, and Linguistics 41 (= *IJAL* 32, 2).
        Bloomington, Ind. etc.
Bierwisch, Manfred
1966   'Regeln für die Intonation deutscher Sätze'. *Studia Grammatica* 7, 99-
        201.
Binnick, Robert I., a.o. (eds.)
1969   *Papers from the fifth regional meeting of the Chicago Linguistic Society*.
        Chicago.

147

Black, Max
    1949   'Vagueness, an exercise in logical analysis'. In: *Language and philosophy;
              studies in method*. Ithaca N.Y., 23-58.
    1952   'Ambiguity'. In: *Critical thinking*. New York, 167-81.
Bloch, Bernard
    1941   'Phonemic overlapping'. *AS* 16, 278-84. Quoted from: Joos 1957, 93-6.
    1948   'A set of postulates for phonemic analysis'. *Lg* 24, 3-46.
Bloch, Bernard and George L.Trager
    1942   *Outline of linguistic analysis*. Baltimore.
Bloomfield, Leonard
    1935   *Language*. London.
Bolinger, Dwight L.
    1958   'A theory of pitch accent in English'. *Word* 14, 109-19. Quoted from:
              Bolinger 1965b, 17-55.
    1961a   'Contrastive accent and contrastive stress'. *Lg* 37, 83-96. Quoted from:
              Bolinger 1965b, 101-117.
    1961b   *Generality, gradience, and the all-or-none*. Janua Linguarum, series
              minor, 14. The Hague.
    1961c   'Syntactic blends and other matters'. *Lg* 37, 366-81.
    1965a   'The atomization of meaning'. *Lg* 41, 555-73.
    1965b   *Forms of English; accent, morpheme, order*. Cambridge, Mass., etc.
    1968   'Adjectives in English: attribution and predication'. *Lingua* 18, 1-34.
Bolinger, Dwight L. and Louis J.Gerstman
    1957   'Disjuncture as a cue to constructs'. *Word* 13, 246-55. Quoted from:
              Bolinger 1965b, 85-93.
Booth, Wayne C.
    1966[6]   *The rhetoric of fiction*. Chicago etc.

Callow, John C.
    1968   'A hierarchical study of neutralization in Kasem'. *JL* 4, 33-45.
Cantineau, J.
    1952   'Les oppositions significatives'. *CFS* 10, 11-40.
Chao, Yuen Ren
    1959   'Ambiguity in Chinese'. In: *Studia serica Bernhard Karlgren dedicata*.
              Copenhagen 1959, 1-13.
Chomsky, Noam
    1955a   *The logical structure of linguistic theory*. Cambridge, Mass. Unpub-
              lished; mimeographed.
    1955b   'Semantic considerations in grammar'. *Monographs on Languages and
              Linguistics* 8, 141-58. Washington.
    1957   *Syntactic structures*. Janua Linguarum, series minor 4. The Hague.
    1963   'Formal properties of grammars'. In: Luce, Bush and Galanter 1963,
              323-418.
    1964   *Current issues in linguistic theory*. Janua Linguarum, series minor 38.
              The Hague, etc.
    1965   *Aspects of the theory of syntax*. Cambridge, Mass.
    1966   *Cartesian linguistics: a chapter in the history of rationalist thought*.
              New York, etc.

1967a   'The formal nature of language'. In: Lenneberg 1967, 397-442.
1967b   'Some general properties of phonological rules'. *Lg* 43, 102-28.
1970   'Remarks on nominalization'. In: Jacobs and Rosenbaum 1970, 184-221.
unp.   'Deep structure, surface structure, and semantic interpretation'. Cambridge, Mass. Preliminary version.

Chomsky, Noam and Morris Halle
     1965   'Some controversial questions in phonological theory'. *JL* 1, 95-138.
     1968   *The sound pattern of English*. New York, etc.

Chomsky, Noam and George A.Miller
     1963   'Introduction to the formal analysis of natural languages'. In: Luce, Bush and Galanter 1963, 269-321.

Chomsky, Noam, Morris Halle, and F.Lukoff
     1956   'On accent and juncture in English'. In: Halle a.o. 1956, 65-80.

Cohen, A. and J. 't Hart
     1967   'On the anatomy of intonation'. *Lingua* 19, 177-92.

Dik, Simon C.
     1968a   *Coordination; its implications for the theory of general linguistics*. Amsterdam.
     1968b   'Referential identity'. *Lingua* 21, 70-97.

Dougherty, Ray C.
     1967   *Coordinate conjunction*. PEGS paper 10, November 14, 1967.

Empson, William
     1965   *Seven types of ambiguity*. Harmondsworth, etc. First published 1930.

Fillmore, Charles J.
     1966   'Deictic categories in the semantics of 'come'.' *FL* 2, 219-27.
     1968   'The case for case'. In: Bach and Harms 1968, 1-88.
     1969   'Toward a modern theory of case'. In: Reibel and Schane 1969, 361-75. First published 1966.

Flores d'Arcais, G.B. and W.J.M.Levelt (eds.)
     1970   *Advances in psycholinguistics*. Research papers presented at the Bressanone Conference on Psycholinguistics 1969. Amsterdam.

Fodor, Jerry J. and Jerrold J.Katz (eds.)
     1964   *The structure of language*. Readings in the philosophy of language. Englewood Cliffs, N.J.

Garrett, Merrill F.
     1970   'Does ambiguity complicate the perception of sentences?' In: Flores d'Arcais and Levelt 1970, 48-60.

Garvin, Paul L.
     1968   'The place of heuristics in the Fulcrum approach to machine translation'. *Lingua* 21, 162-82.

Gleason, H.A., Jr.
     1965   *Linguistics and English grammar*. New York, etc.

Godel, Robert
    1948   'Homonymie et identité'. *CFS* 7, 5-15. Quoted from: Hamp, House-
                holder, and Austerlitz 1966, 192-98.
Greenberg, Joseph H.
    1966a[2]   'Some universals of grammar with particular reference to the order of
                meaningful elements'. In: Greenberg 1966b[2], 73-113.
Greenberg, Joseph H. (ed.)
    1966b[2]   *Universals of language.* Cambridge, Mass.
Greibach, Sheila A.
    1963   'The undecidability of the ambiguity problem for minimal linear gram-
                mars'. *Information and Control* 6, 119-25.

Haas, W.
    1957   'Zero in linguistic description'. In: *Studies in linguistic analysis*; Special
                number of the Philological Society, 33-53. Oxford.
Halle, Morris
    1964   'Phonology in generative grammar'. In: Fodor and Katz 1964, 334-52.
                First published in *Word* 18 (1962), 54-72.
Halle, Morris a.o. (eds.)
    1956   *For Roman Jakobson*; essays on the occasion of his sixtieth birthday.
                The Hague.
Hamp, Eric P., Fred W.Householder, and Robert Austerlitz (eds.)
    1966   *Readings in linguistics 2.* Chicago, etc.
Harman, Gilbert
    1966   'About what an adequate grammar could do'. *FL* 2, 134-41.
Harris, Zellig S.
    1963[6]   *Structural linguistics.* Chicago, etc. First published 1951 as *Methods in
                structural linguistics.*
Haugen, Einar
    1956   'The syllable in linguistic description'. In: Halle a.o. 1956, 213-221.
Hjelmslev, Louis
    1939   'Note sur les oppositions supprimables'. *TCLP* 8, 51-7.
    1961   *Prolegomena to a theory of language.* Transl. by Francis J. Whitfield.
                Madison. First published 1943.
Hoard, J.E.
    1966   'Juncture and syllable structure in English'. *Phonetica* 15, 96-109.
Hockett, Charles F.
    1954   'Two models of grammatical description'. *Word* 10, 210-31. Quoted
                from: Joos 1957, 387-99.
    1958   *A course in modern linguistics.* New York.
    1961   'Grammar for the hearer'. In: Jakobson 1961, 220-36.
    1966   'What Algonquian is really like'. *IJAL* 32, 59-73.
Householder, F.
    1965   'Some recent claims in phonological theory'. *JL* 1, 13-34.
Hudson, R.A.
    1970   'On clauses containing conjoined and plural noun phrases in English'.
                Lingua 24, 205-53.

Jackendoff, Ray S.
1968   *An interpretive theory of pronouns and reflexives.* PEGS papers 27,
             April 1968.
Jacobs, Roderick A. and Peter S.Rosenbaum (eds.)
1970   *Readings in English transformational grammar.* Waltham, Mass.
Jakobson, Roman (ed.)
1961   *Structure of language and its mathematical aspects.* Proceedings of
             symposia in applied mathematics 12. Providence.
Jespersen, Otto
1964[12]   *Language; its nature, development, and origin.* London. First published
             1922.
Joos, Martin (ed.)
1957   *Readings in linguistics; the development of descriptive linguistics in
             America since 1925.* Washington.

Kaplan, Abraham
1950   'An experimental study of ambiguity and context'. The RAND cor-
             poration. Santa Monica, Calif. Mimeographed.
Katz, Jerrold J.
1964   'Semantic theory and the meaning of 'good'.' *The Journal of Philosophy*
             61, 739-66.
1966   *The philosophy of language.* New York, etc.
1967   'Recent issues in semantic theory'. *FL* 3, 124-94.
Katz, Jerrold J. and Jerry A.Fodor
1964   'The structure of a semantic theory'. In: Fodor and Katz 1964, 479-
             518. First published in *Lg* 39 (1963), 170–210.
Katz, Jerrold J. and Paul M.Postal
1964   *An integrated theory of linguistic descriptions.* Cambridge Mass.
Kim, Chin-Wu
1968   Review of Lieberman 1967. *Lg* 44, 830-42.
Kraak, A.
1966   *Negatieve zinnen; een methodologische en grammatische analyse.*
             Hilversum.
Kuno, Susumu and Anthony G.Oettinger
1963   'Syntactic structure and ambiguity in English'. In: AFIPS Conference
             Proceedings 24, 397-418. Baltimore, etc.
Kuryłowicz, J.
1964   *The inflectional categories of Indo-European.* Heidelberg.

Lakoff, George
1968   'Instrumental adverbs and the concept of deep structure'. *FL* 4, 4-29.
Lamb, Sydney M.
1964   'The sememic approach to structural semantics'. *American Anthropol-
             ogist* 66, 57-78.
1966   *Outline of stratificational grammar.* Washington.
Lees, Robert B.
1960   'A multiply ambiguous adjectival construction in English'. *Lg* 36,
             207-21.

152   BIBLIOGRAPHY

1966[4]   *The grammar of English nominalizations.* Indiana Univ. Research
            Center in Anthropology, Folklore, and Linguistics 12. Bloomington,
            etc. First published 1960.
Lehiste, Ilse
1960   *An acoustic-phonetic study of internal open juncture.* Basel, etc. Suppl.
            to *Phonetica* 5.
Lenneberg, Eric H.
1967   *Biological foundations of language.* New York, etc.
Leopold, Werner F.
1948   'German *ch'. Lg* 24, 179-80. Quoted from Joos 1957, 215-6.
Lieberman, Philip
1965   'On the accoustic basis of the perception of intonation by linguists'.
            Word 21, 40-54.
1967   *Intonation, perception, and language.* Cambridge, Mass.
Lu, John H.T.
1965   *Contrastive stress and emphatic stress.* Ohio State University Research
            Foundation, Project on linguistic analysis, report 10.
Luce, Duncan R., Robert R.Bush, and Eugene Galanter
1963   *Handbook of mathematical psychology*, Vol. 2. New York, etc.
Lyons, John
1968   *Introduction to theoretical linguistics.* Cambridge.

MacKay, D.G.
1966   'To end ambiguous sentences'. *Perception and Psychophysics* 1, 426-36.
MacKay, Donald G. and Thomas G.Bever
1967   'In search of ambiguity'. *Perception and Psychophysics* 2, 193-200.
Malécot, André and Paul Lloyd
1967   'The /t/ : /d/ distinction in American alveolar flaps'. *Lingua* 18, 168-78.
Malkiel, Y.
1959   'Studies in irreversible binomials'. *Lingua* 8, 113-60.
Malmberg, Bertil
1944   'La coupe syllabique dans le système consonantique du français'. *AL* 4,
            61-6.
1964   'Juncture and syllable division'. In: Abercrombie a.o. 1964, 116-9.
Mandelbaum, David G. (ed.)
1949   *Selected writings of Edward Sapir in language, culture, and personality.*
            Berkeley, etc.
Martinet, André a.o.
1957   *La notion de neutralisation dans la morphologie et le lexique.* (= *TILP*
            2). Paris.
Martinet, André
1962   *A functional view of language..*Oxford.
McCawley, James D.
1968a   'The rôle of semantics in a grammar'. In: Bach and Harms 1968, 125-
            69.
1968b   Review of Sebeok 1966. *Lg* 44, 556-93.
1970   'Where do noun phrases come from?' In: Jacobs and Rosenbaum 1970,
            166-83.

Mok, Q.I.M.
1968a   *Contribution à l'étude des catégories morphologiques du genre et du nombre dans le français parlé actuel*. The Hague.
1968b   'Vaugelas et la 'désambiguïsation' de la parole'. *Lingua* 21, 303-11.
Mol. H. and E.M.Uhlenbeck
1956   'The linguistic relevance of intensity in stress'. *Lingua* 5, 205-213.
Moulton, William G.
1947   'Juncture in modern standard German'. *Lg* 23, 212-26. Quoted from: Joos 1957, 208-15.

Newmeyer, Frederick
1969   'The underlying structure of the *begin*-class verbs'. In: Binnick a.o. 1969, 195-203.
Nida, Eugene A.
1948   'The identification of morphemes'. *Lg* 24, 414-41. Quoted from: Joos 1957, 255-71.

O'Connor, J.D. and Olive M.Tooley
1964   'The perceptibility of certain word-boundaries'. In: Abercrombie a.o. 1964, 171-6.

Pike, Kenneth L.
1963   'Theoretical implications of matrix permutation in Fore (New Guinea)'. *AnL* 5:8, 1-23.
1967²   *Language in relation to a unified theory of the structure of human behavior*. Janua Linguarum, series maior 24. The Hague, etc.
Pike, Kenneth L. and Barbara Erickson
1964   'Conflated field structures in Potawatomi and Arabic'. *IJAL* 30, 201-12.
Postal, Paul M.
1968   *Aspects of phonological theory*. New York, etc.
Puhvel, Jaan (ed.)
1969   *Substance and structure of language*. Berkeley, etc.

Quine, Willard Van Orman
1964²   *Word and object*. Cambridge, Mass.
Quintilian, M.Fabius
         Institutio oratoria, VI, VII. Transl. by H.E.Butler. London, etc. 1959.

Reddy, Michael
1969   'A semantic approach to metaphor'. In: Binnick a.o. 1969, 240-50.
Reibel, David A. and Sanford A. Schane (eds.).
1969   *Modern studies in English; readings in transformational grammar*. Englewood Cliffs, N.J.
Reichling, Anton
1935   *Het woord; een studie omtrent de grondslag van taal en taalgebruik*. Nijmegen.
1939   *Over essentiële en toevallige grammatica-regels*. Public address University of Amsterdam. Groningen.

154   BIBLIOGRAPHY

1969[5]   Verzamelde studies over hedendaagse problemen der taalwetenschap.
             Zwolle.
Robins, R.H.
    1959   'In defence of WP'. TPS 1959, 116-44. Quoted from: Robins 1970,
             47-77.
    1970   Diversions of Bloomsbury; selected writings on linguistics. North-
             Holland Linguistic Series. Amsterdam.
Ruipérez, Martin S.
    1953   'The neutralization of morphological oppositions as illustrated by the
             neutral aspect of the present indicative in Classical Greek'. Word 9,
             241-52.

Sapir, Edward
    1925   'Sound patterns in language'. Lg 1, 37-51. Quoted from: Joos 1957,
             19-31.
    1949   'The psychological reality of phonemes'. In: Mandelbaum 1949, 46-60.
             First published 1933.
Schwartz, Arthur
    1968   'Derivative functions in syntax'. Lg 44, 747-83.
Sebeok, Thomas A. (ed.)
    1966   Current trends in linguistics 3: theoretical foundations. The Hague.
Sharp, A.E.
    1960   'The analysis of stress and juncture in English'. TPS, 104-35.
Smith, Carlota S.
    1964   'Determiners and relative clauses in a generative grammar of English'.
             Lg 40, 37-52.
Smith, Henry Lee, Jr.
    1956   Linguistic science and the teaching of English. Cambridge, Mass.
Stern, Gustav
    1931   Meaning and change of meaning; with special reference to the English
             language. Reissued 1964 in: Indiana University Studies in the History
             and Theory of Linguistics, Bloomington.
Stockwell, Robert P.
    1962   Intervention in First Texas Conference on problems of linguistic anal-
             ysis in English 1957, p. 44 ff. Austin, Texas.
Stutterheim, C.F.P.
    1965[2]   Taalbeschouwing en taalbeheersing. Amsterdam. First published 1954.
Sutherland, Robert D.
    1970   Language and Lewis Carroll. Janua Linguarum, series maior 26. The
             Hague.

Trager, George L. and Henry Lee Smith Jr.
    1951   Outline of English structure. Norman, Oklahoma.
Trubetzkoy, N.S.
    1939   Grundzüge der Phonologie. Göttingen.

Ullmann, Stephen
    1962   Semantics; an introduction to the science of meaning. Oxford.

Weinreich, Uriel
  1964   'Webster's Third: a critique of its semantics'. *IJAL* 30, 405-9.
  1966a   'On the semantic structure of language'. In: Greenberg 1966b[2], 142-216.
  1966b   'Explorations in semantic theory'. In: Sebeok 1966, 395-477.
  1969   'Problems in the analysis of idioms'. In: Puhvel 1969, 23-81.
Wells, Rulon
  1947   'Immediate constituents'. *Lg* 23, 81-117. Quoted from: Joos 1957, 186-207.
Wonder, J.P.
  1970   'Ambiguity and the English gerund'. *Lingua* 25, 254-67.

Ziff, Paul
  1964   *Semantic analysis*. Ithaca N.Y.
  1965   'About what an adequate grammar couldn't do'. *FL* 1, 5-13.
Zimmer, Karl E.
  1968   Review of Chomsky 1966. *IJAL* 34, 290-303.

SUBJECT INDEX

Accidental vs. purposive, 80-3
Adnominal possessive, 100, 108-9
Ambiguity
   and generality, 119-21, 126*n*
   and grammar, 57 ff.
   and levels of description, 8ff., 11-4,
      19-20, 23, 27-9, 32, 88
   and linguistic specification, 101-2,
      110-11, 114-5, 141, 146
   and literature, 4, 121-3
   and neutrality, 70, 94-9, 105-7
   and orthography, 9
   and phonology, 11 ff.
   and probability, 9, 23-5, 36-7, 111-5,
      136-7
   and proper names, 5
   and the lexicon, 111-5, 117 ff.
   and the perception of sentences, 16,
      21, 23-4, 27-8, 36-8, 43, 55, 60-1
   and vagueness, 93, 99-101, 118-9,
      126*n*
   as a heuristic tool, 89, 93, 94*n*, 102,
      133-7
   by supposition, 120*n*
   contextual –, 3-6, 121-3, 126
   general definition of –, 1
   inherent in natural language, 1, 3-4
   inherent vs. non inherent –, 3, 6-7,
      106, 108, 117-8, 121-3
   kinds of –, 108-10, 117
   linguistic definition of –, 5 ff.
   vs. homonymy, 6, 8, 60-1, 72 ff.,
      97-99, 105-6
   vs. polysemy, 6, 117-8, 133-46
Anaphoric reference, 59, 107

Breath-group, 50-1

Case grammar, 88*n*
Competence, 134-7
Content, 117-8
Contextual specialization, 137-41
Constructional homonymy, 2, 45, 63-7,
   72

Co-occurrence, 73-4, 75 ff.
Coordination, 2, 54, 63-5, 111-2
   and plurality, 65

Definite noun phrases, 53-4, 96-9, 113-4
Deep structure, 45-6, 62, 74-6, 78, 83,
   85*n*, 86, 88, 101, 106-7
Disambiguation
   and grammatical constraints, 113-4
   and intonation, 46-8, 52-3, 55
   and juncture, 3, 36-38
   and semantic imcompatibility, 134-7
Disjuncture, 16, 36
Diversification, 63, 94*n*

Ergative, 57, 103

Generality, 119-21, 126*n*
Gesamtbedeutung, 89, 92

Homomorphic, 10, 63*n*
Homonymy, 1-2, 8, 60-1, 103-5, 108,
   111
   and grammatical description, 57 ff.,
      64-7, 72
   and constituent structure, 2, 67-72
   as a heuristic tool, 62-4
   and lexical description, 58, 62, 124-6
   and idiom, 128
Homophony, 7, 11, 63*n*
Hyponymy, 119-20

IC-analysis, 63-5
Idiom, 126-7
Instrumental adverbs, 79-84, 92-3, 112-5
Interpretation, 117-8, 141-6
Intonation, 10, 14-5, 55, 59
   contrastive, 42-8
   emphatic, 42-8
   and syntactic structure, 38-42
   and thematic function, 46-8

Juncture
   and Dutch compounds, 33-4

AUTHOR INDEX

159